wl

A LAYMAN'S GUIDE
TO UNITED KINGDOM AIR
TRAFFIC CONTROL

A LAYMAN'S GUIDE TO UNITED KINGDOM AIR TRAFFIC CONTROL

Dave Graves

Airlife
England

First published in the UK 1989
by Airlife Publishing Ltd.

British Library Cataloguing in Publication Data available.

ISBN 1 85310 078 1 (Cased)
ISBN 1 85310 107 9 (Paperback)

Printed in England by Livesey Ltd., Shrewsbury.

Airlife Publishing Ltd.

101 Longden Road, Shrewsbury, England.

Contents

Writing a book about ATC should be a fairly straightforward exercise for an Air Traffic Control Officer. The job is really all about the application of rules, regulations and procedures which are set out in the basic Manual of Air Traffic Services (MATS), the MATS Part 2 in which each ATC unit publishes procedures which apply to that particular unit, and various Aeronautical Information Publications, not forgetting the Air Navigation Act. However, these documents don't make good reading.

One's own experience can help to provide interest but no one can know everything about all the airports and ATC units in the country. Help was required in the provision of drawings and of background and historical information and I approached the Civil Aviation Authority for permission to use or adapt various drawings such as airport plans and some charts of the London Area, as well as the airport operators for handbooks, timetables, road access maps, flight enquiry telephone numbers, etc.

I would like to express my gratitude to the authorities who provided information or who gave me permission to use published drawings. They are listed below.

In particular I thank the PROs who were kind enough to check lists of airline users and flight enquiry telephone numbers and to update them where necessary. My thanks also to the ATC personnel at the airports who advised me of any changes of procedure.

Any opinions in the book are my own.

Acknowledgements

The Civil Aviation Authority; Birmingham International Airport plc; East Midlands International Airport plc; Gatwick Airport Ltd; Glasgow Airport (Scottish Airports Ltd); Heathrow Airport Ltd; Leeds/Bradford Airport Ltd; Liverpool Airport plc; London City Airport (John Mowlem & Co); Luton International Airport Ltd; Manchester Airport plc; Newcastle International Airport Ltd.

And to Geoff Parkes, my draughtsman, who accepted some awful scribbles from me and turned them into real drawings. Also to No 223 Area Radar Course.

Foreword

Travellers on road transport usually have a good idea of what is happening around them and know all about such things as traffic lights, motorways, major and minor roads, roundabouts and their various rules and regulations. But to the air traveller the Air Traffic Control system is invariably something of a mystery.

Even to those not travelling, aircraft have a fascination and many thousands of people visit our airports every year, some even making a day of it. They wander through the terminals, gaze at aircraft taxiing, taking-off and landing and many carry radios and listen in to the control tower. The visitors obviously find all the activity very interesting but very few seem to understand it. Probably most would like to visit the tower but hordes of people wandering through would be too much of a distraction for controllers and, so, Air Traffic Control is out of bounds to the public.

This book sets out to explain the methods by which pilots find their way about the skies from take-off to touchdown, how radar is used by ATC to see and control the aircraft and how communications are maintained. It shows the procedures used by ATC at British airports, both in the air and on the ground, and how these airports fit into the wider context of the United Kingdom ATC system. It is not a textbook and it certainly won't help you to become an Air Traffic Control Officer; it is merely a guide for passengers (and visitors).

Throughout, the ATC procedures are explained in familiar terms and made to apply, where possible, to basic situations. If the world of ATC is a mystery and the control tower is out of bounds, this book will answer many of the questions the airline passenger or airport visitor might wish to ask.

We are looking at quite a big empire. Most people know of the major airports, all of which will be described, but we can also see what happens at some of the regional airports. Not everyone is aware that the biggest ATC unit in the country is not at an airport at all, exists solely to control airspace and routes not in the immediate vicinity of airports and will be involved in the control of most passenger and freight-carrying flights. We can see how this operates.

It will all be easier to understand if the book is divided into six parts. Part 1 gives basic information necessary for the understanding of expressions and abbreviations used later. Parts 2 and 3 deal separately with the London area airports and en-route control and the airports to the north of London with the airspace and control procedures in that area as far north as the Scottish border. Part 4 looks at Scottish airspace and Glasgow airport. Part 5 is a supplement which explains how to get to or from the various airports using either public or private transport, where to park the car, etc, and also gives lists of user airlines with their flight prefixes and flight enquiry telephone numbers. Part 6 consists of an Author's Note and some appendices.

As the book progresses the Air Traffic Control detail is considerably reduced in favour of more background interest. This is not an attempt to grade airports but merely to avoid a catalogue effect. Having dealt fully with Heathrow and Gatwick it would be boring to repeat similar details for the other airports, all of which operate under the same rules and use the same procedures, albeit with different patterns to suit their own aerodromes or airspace. The reader interested in an airport other than Heathrow or Gatwick is advised to read Part 1 followed by the chapters on the major airports before going on to his or her particular interest. It should also be noted that airways control is dealt with in Parts 2, 3, and 4 for the different areas covered.

There are three subjects of interest which do not fit naturally into any of Parts 1 to 6. Flow control, aircraft noise and flights across the North Atlantic are, therefore, included in Part 2 because it is felt that they are relevant to ATC procedures in general and should be in fairly prominent positions in the book.

Altitudes and heights at which aircraft fly are referred to in feet throughout the book but there will be some who know that 'Flight Levels' are also used in practice. An explanation is provided in Appendix 1.

It is hoped that this book helps to dispel the mystery associated with ATC and that readers will acquire a familiarity with airports which will make air travel a more enjoyable experience.

Introduction

Flying. Some like it but many people are nervous about it. But more of us are doing it and it is estimated that by 1995 Heathrow will be handling 38 million passengers per year, Gatwick 25 million and Luton 3½ million. And the regional airports?

That's an awful lot of passengers. They first have the hassle of getting to the airport, then finding where to check in. They wait for announcements and queue for refreshments. Some have children. Who has the tickets? Where are the passports? Is that delay being announced for us? And then they get on to the aircraft and sit. And wait. What is it all about?

And when they do get airborne, more trauma. How does the pilot know where to go? Who is looking after us? Are we likely to have a collision? Why didn't we go back to Bournemouth this year?

Don't worry. There is a whole profession dedicated to the safety of aircraft from the time they start their engines at the departure airport until they park at the destination. It is called Air Traffic Control (ATC) and its members are highly trained and very efficient. Air Traffic Control Officers (ATCOs) undergo long periods of basic training to qualify for provisional licences to operate, but the licences do not entitle them to provide an ATC service at a particular airport or ATC Centre. To do that they have to carry out further local training under instruction and then take even more examinations to show that they have the ability to control aircraft at that unit before having their licences endorsed to that effect and being allowed to work alone. Every twelve months they have to pass the same medical examination as pilots; if they fail that medical their licences are suspended.

Civil ATC operates within what is called Controlled or Special Rules Airspace which is airspace within which aircraft are not permitted to fly without ATC permission. It is designed to provide protection for aircraft down to ground level in the vicinity of airports and at higher levels for the routes between airports, and the regulations are enforceable by law. The procedures used by ATC are agreed internationally by the International Civil Aviation Organization (ICAO) and, although this books deals with the United Kingdom, procedures in other countries will be very much the same.

ATC is not a complicated science. Just as in any other transport system its purpose is to prevent two or more aircraft (trains, cars, buses) being in the same place at the same time. Computers are used for passing information quickly and for some routine things such as estimating time of flight between various points, but control is the responsibility of human controllers who will not cease to function when a fuse blows. It follows that the system must be logical and straightforward and within the capability of men and women to operate.

ATC is about the regulation and control of air traffic within that human capability. Because of the high speeds involved, the fact that it all happens in space, and because aircraft in the air cannot be stopped, the procedures must be different but, if you can understand the road traffic system, you will find that the ATC system is equally reasonable although much more disciplined. What it boils down to is safety, and it works.

STOP PRESS. In October 1988 the CAA (Civil Aviation Authority) announced that it was to spend £600m over ten years to improve the facilities available to ATC with the provision of new radars, computers and communications systems. However, this will not alter the fact that the decisions will still have to be made by controllers.

Part 1

In Part 1 we can look at the means of communication between pilots and ATC and see how pilots can find their way and then land in bad weather. There is also a brief description of radar, a basic ATC tool, and an explanation of controlled airspace as well as a preliminary consideration of the various types of ATC units (they are not all at airports).

This part should be read with a view to understanding the descriptions and explanations that follow in Parts 2, 3 and 4.

Chapter 1
The Tools of the Trade

Advances in aviation have come about not only because of improvements in the technical standards of aircraft. What were once considered the barriers of distance, speed and the ability to fly at higher altitudes and above much of the weather have been largely overcome because of these improvements, and a flight to Australia which would once have taken a week or more with many stops can now be completed in 28 hours with only two stops for refuelling. But none of this could have happened without significant improvements in the means by which pilots find their way about the skies and the establishment of a world-wide ATC system to regulate the flow of air traffic so as to ensure its safety.

The art of finding the way from one place to another is called 'navigation' and there was a time when airlines carried specialist navigators. However, developments in radio aids to navigation mean that pilots can now carry out this function and navigators are seldom carried except in remote areas. Radio is not just a means of communication in aviation, it can also be used to show the pilot his position, to help him to follow a route accurately and to enable him to land in weather conditions which would have made it quite unthinkable just a few years ago. For ATC radio is a means of passing information and instructions and even to 'see' the positions of aircraft on a radar screen.

These radio devices all have their names which are everyday expressions in aviation but are unfamiliar to the general public. The jargon concerning the tools of the trade contributes to the mystery of ATC so we must first understand what radio aids to navigation and ATC are all about and we can also look briefly at the lighting systems which help pilots to operate in poor weather and at night. Some of this may seem a little dull but it is necessary to understand the basics before going on to the operational aspects.

Very High Frequency Radio Telephone (VHF RT)
In the early days of aviation there was no communication between pilots and aerodrome authorities other than lamp signals when the aircraft were on the ground or very close to the aerodrome. An aircraft flying from London to Paris in those days would have set

off just as sailing ships used to between ports with nothing but silence between departure and arrival. The first sign of trouble could have been its non-arrival or, with luck, a telephone call from the pilot to say that he had force-landed.

As things developed, some aircraft were able to carry radio sets and wireless operators but, even then, they had to pass messages in Morse code which were written down and passed by an operator between the pilot and the aerodrome authority. Any reply had to be written for the wireless operator to transmit. Ships used the same procedure; it was slow and cumbersome but better than nothing.

The advent of Radio Telephone (RT) was an enormous advance enabling the pilot to speak directly to people on the ground. Not only was it very convenient, it also improved the safety factor because aircraft could be controlled much more easily, and given advice and assistance more quickly. The original RT sets were large and heavy and not too dependable but modern sets are reliable and light-weight and only a very few, mainly private, aircraft fly without radio.

It is not too long ago that our home radio sets began to use the Very High Frequency (VHF) band for a higher standard of reception. Aviation had used VHF for many years before that, largely because high quality transmission and reception are essential for the task.

In the same way that different radio stations (BBC, LBC, Capital, etc) use different frequencies so that they will not interfere with each other, ATC uses different frequencies for different purposes or for different aerodromes (Dia 1.1). Aircraft, or even vehicles, using Heathrow Airport must be on a different frequency from aircraft approaching Heathrow under radar control, and Gatwick and Luton must have their own frequencies for their different purposes. ATCOs can simply select a pre-set frequency (or 'channel') which is allocated for a particular function, for example Ground Movement Control which is the control of all aircraft and vehicles moving on the airport other than those landing or taking-off, while pilots have multi-channel radios on which they can select any VHF frequency.

The practical difference between RT and ordinary telephones is that RT channels are 'open' and any number of people can be on the frequency at the same time. There is a danger of confusion and, to avoid this, every user has a call sign and every transmission must be 'addressed'.

The various ATC units are identified by both the location and the particular function, eg, 'Heathrow Tower' and 'Heathrow

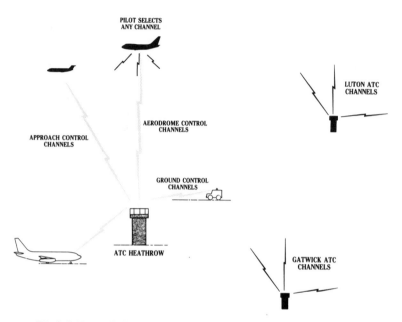

Dia 1.1 Typical allocation of ATC VHF/RT channels (frequencies).

Approach'. Aircraft usually will use either their aircraft registration (which in the UK consists of five letters which are spoken phonetically as explained later), or the flight number which you will have on your ticket. But there are slight differences even then because some operators will use the company name as an RT callsign while others use a codeword. So 'BAL' on your ticket becomes 'Britannia' but 'BAW' becomes 'Speedbird', the British Airways RT callsign.

The RT language used worldwide is English, although some countries may use their own language in addition. It follows that many pilots and controllers are using a language which is not their own and so, to avoid misunderstanding, standard words and expressions are laid down by ICAO for use on RT and these must be used at all times. Pilots and controllers will recognize and understand these expected words and expressions more easily and this is obviously safer. Not for ATC the hurly-burly of Citizen's Band radio; the name of this game is RT discipline.

For brevity as well as clarity certain code-words are used in ATC. Some examples are:

Roger: I have received all of your last transmission.

Wilco: Your message received, understood and will be complied with.
Over: My transmission is ended and I expect a reply.
Out: This conversation is ended. I do not expect a reply.
Cleared to: This is a combined ATC permission/instruction as in 'Cleared to take-off'.
Hold: Wait/stay where you are.

We all know that the letters of the alphabet can be confused. For example, B, C, D, E, G, P, T and V can all sound much the same and so, ATC uses a phonetic alphabet and those letters are pronounced as Bravo, Charlie, Delta, Echo, Golf, Papa, Tango and Victor, and all the other letters have their own phonetics.

So much for the method of communication and the language of ATC. The navigation equipment used in aviation is also approved and standardised by ICAO and we can look now at those used in ATC. It may not be easy to understand that a radio beacon or a radio landing aid can be received and interpreted by an aircraft receiver in such a way that a pilot can navigate or land through cloud or fog, but if we remember that a colour TV picture is just an interpretation of a radio signal we can, I think, accept it. ATCOs have to understand how these things work but laymen do not need to any more than they need to understand television.

Radar
Radar is an acronym for Radio Detection and Ranging. It enables the controller to 'see' the aircraft under his control in the form of blips of light on a dark screen and the radar technicians can also display such things as maps of coastlines or of particular airspace boundaries so that the controller can relate the radar blips to the aircraft's position over land or sea, to a particular air route or to an aerodrome. Since the controller can also see the position of aircraft relative to each other, he can issue instructions to keep them separated; he will know when it is safe to turn or climb or descend or, equally important, when it is not safe to do so. In the days before radar aircraft were separated by either time or altitude, but radar has enabled controllers to speed up the system with no loss of safety.

In absolutely non-technical terms a radar system comprises a large 'dish-shaped' transmitting/receiving aerial which rotates at about ten times per minute, a lot of electronics and a radar screen (or screens). The transmitter and receiver operate alternately in very, very short bursts measured in thousandths of a second while the aerial rotates. The transmitter punches out a radio beam at the speed of light (186,000 miles per second) and switches off. The receiver switches on and receives the reflection of the radio beam from any object in its path. Transmit, receive, transmit, receive — each for thousandths of a second (Dia 1.2).

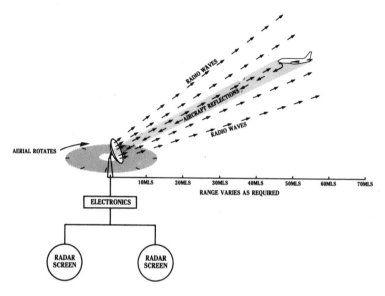

Dia 1.2. How radar works.

As the radar reflections are received the precise direction from the aerial is measured by the electronics and the time from transmit to receive is also measured to give the distance. In addition, any object which is stationary such as a building is recognized as such. The electronics then 'paint' on the radar screen only the moving objects like aircraft together with any map superimposed by the technicians. As the aircraft moves the blips also move across the screen leaving a tail of decreasing light (the afterglow) from which the controller can assess direction and approximate speed. Where the radar displays are computer-processed the tail is shown by a trail of dots.

That describes what is called 'primary radar'. Some years ago 'secondary radar' was developed for use with primary. It transmits in the same way but this transmission is received by a receiver in the aircraft, an aircraft transmitter is 'triggered' and this sends back to the aerial details of the aircraft callsign, altitude and destination which are then displayed on the radar screen alongside the primary radar blips (Dia 1.3). This system is very useful indeed to controllers because it identifies each blip and makes the display three-dimensional (Dia 1.4 shows the difference) and it enables other controllers to see what is happening without having to ask for a detailed explanation. The secondary radar system is capable of further development to pass much more information automatically and this will, of course, reduce talking time and allow more thinking time for controllers.

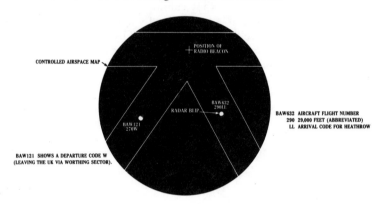

Dia 1.3. The radar screen showing radar map with primary and secondary radar.

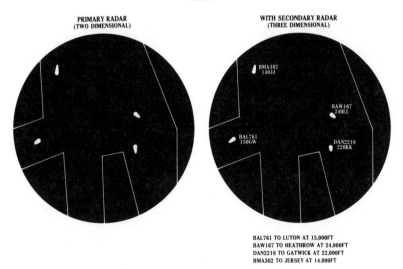

Dia 1.4. Typical radar displays.

VHF Omni-directional Range (VOR)

The expression 'VHF Omni-directional Range' is enough to make the mind boggle but it is always referred to as a VOR and its purpose is to indicate to a pilot his direction from a radio beacon in degrees.

There are various means by which a pilot can navigate his aircraft; this is one of them and the type most commonly used worldwide. Pilots need navigational assistance because their aircraft drift with the wind, they cannot always assess the amount of drift accurately and, of course, they fly in cloud and cannot see where they are relative to the ground. A VOR enables the pilot to establish his aircraft on a precise line (or track) and to follow a route without having to worry about drift or visibility.

The VOR is a VHF radio beacon which transmits signals in all directions (ie, through 360°) which are received in the aircraft (Dia 1.5). The transmissions vary very slightly from one degree to

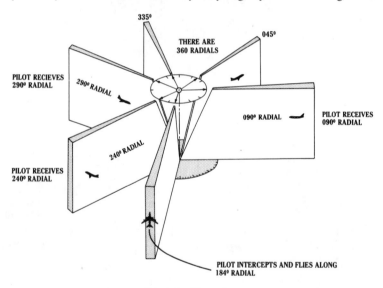

Dia 1.5. The VOR.

another and the aircraft receiver 'recognizes' each different degree and then displays to the pilot his direction in degrees relative to the VOR as well as a to/from indication. The line of each degree from the VOR is called a radial. VORs are positioned along, or at the ends, of routes over land and the routes are then defined along radials from or to the beacon. Thus a pilot can position himself, or be positioned by ATC, on a radial and can then fly that radial to stay on the route.

A pilot uses VORs almost as a car driver uses roads. He can, of course, fly from one VOR to another, staying on specified radials to follow a route. He can select two different VORs and change route by flying towards one until he reaches a specified radial from the second and then turning towards it (Dia 1.6). He can check his position by getting radials from two VORs and drawing them on an aeronautical map on which the VOR positions are shown (Dia 1.7) or by using a VOR radial and a feature such as a coastline.

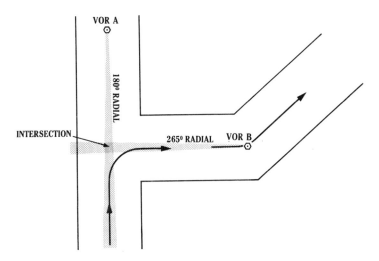

Dia 1.6. Changing route using two VORs.

As you can see, there are several uses for a VOR but the purpose is always more precise navigation. They can operate up to ranges of about 150 miles so a very long air route might require a number of VORs. However, they cannot be sited out to sea and different (internal) navigational aids are used for long sea crossings.

Distance Measuring Equipment (DME)
Having seen how the VOR can be used, it must be said that it would be inconvenient for a pilot along an air route to have to check various positions using two VORs. It was done that way at one time and there are odd occasions when it still is, but most

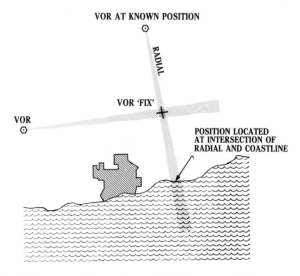

Dia 1.7. Plotting a position using radials from two VORs or one VOR radial and a coastline.

VORs are now associated with a second device called Distance Measuring Equipment (DME).

This also operates through 360° and provides the pilot with his distance from the VOR/DME station (Dia 1.8); he can now read the VOR radial and the DME distance and will know precisely where he is. An air route is established along a VOR radial and the pilot can see at a glance how far he has to fly to reach the VOR and can estimate his time of arrival. If the aircraft is cleared by ATC to climb or descend, the pilot can also be instructed to be at or below a certain altitude by a specified DME distance and he

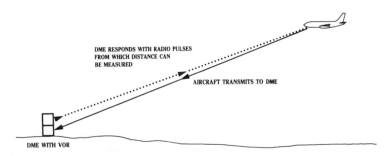

Dia 1.8. Distance measuring equipment.

will then plan his flight accordingly (Dia 1.9). Departure routes from airports are laid down and published in terms of VOR radials and DME ranges, eg, 'Intercept DET VOR radial 260°, cross DET DME20 at 6,000ft'.

Clearly, the addition of DME to VOR means greater precision for both ATC and pilots and it is a very good tool indeed.

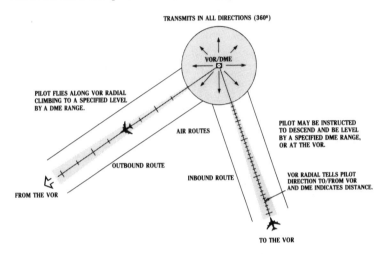

Dia 1.9. Use of combined VOR/DME.

Non-Directional Beacon (NDB)

The NDB is really the forerunner of the VOR. It is a radio beacon which the pilot can fly towards (or away from), or from which he can take a bearing, but there is no provision for giving a distance. A position fix can be obtained by taking bearings from two NDBs but this is rather cumbersome. In the UK, NDBs have a limited use and are generally used as stand-bys for the odd occasions when VORs are switched off for maintenance, to help aircraft from the major airports to follow the initial routes into the ATC system or as 'homing' aids into the smaller airports.

To put it simply, those who own portable radios will know that reception can be improved by turning the set to increase the strength of the signal. This happens because the aerial is self-contained and runs side to side within the cabinet and reception is maximised when the aerial is in line with the transmitting station. The NDB receiver works in much the same way but the direction can be measured in degrees and this information used by pilots as a navigation aid.

Instrument Landing System (ILS)

There is not much point in being able to navigate accurately for distances of up to several thousand miles if at the end of the flight the pilot cannot land his aircraft on a strip of tarmac which may be only fifty yards wide, regardless of the weather. Radio comes to our help once again to provide the pilot with an aid to approach and landing; it is known as the Instrument Landing System (ILS).

When a pilot cannot see the runway he needs a device which will help him to line-up with the runway from a reasonable distance out, say ten miles, so that he can steady the aircraft on the approach path. The first approach aid did just that but added a couple of bleepers at set distances from touch-down; the pilot heard the bleepers (markers) as he flew over them and he knew how far he had to go. He could descend to certain minimum heights after passing the markers but there came a time when he could descend no lower unless he could see the ground. In conditions of low cloud this aid, called the Standard Beam Approach (SBA) and which gave us the expression 'on the beam', was of limited use and something better was needed.

For a while ATC used a radar called Ground Controlled Approach (GCA) in which an ATCO would pass instructions to the pilot to assist him to line-up with the runway and at the same time to descend safely to about 600ft above ground at two miles from touch-down. (Hence the 'talk 'em down' concept that many people have about ATC.) But this, too, was of limited value and certainly was not good enough to enable the airlines to give a reasonable guarantee of maintaining their schedules. Fortunately, improvements were on the way in the shape of the ILS which is now the standard approach and landing aid.

ILS might well have been developed from SBA because it uses the same sort of radio beam to line up the aircraft with the runway but introduces a second beam to indicate the descent path. The markers have been retained as check points at which pilots may be asked to report on final approach (Dia 1.10). The pilot watches an indicator in the cockpit which tells him if he is left or right of the extended centre line of the runway and above or below the ideal descent path (in aviation language this is called the 'Glide Path'). When the pilot eventually sees the approach lights or the runway he should be in just the right position to continue the approach and to land visually.

In fact ILS has been so much refined and improved over the years that it can be coupled to the automatic pilot which can fly the aircraft all the way to the actual landing regardless of the visibility and cloud base. Not all airports are so equipped yet, nor

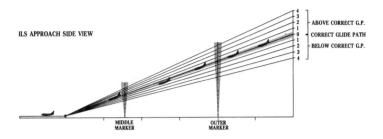

ILS APPROACH SIDE VIEW

ABOVE CORRECT G.P.

CORRECT GLIDE PATH

BELOW CORRECT G.P.

MIDDLE MARKER

OUTER MARKER

ILS APPROACH PLAN VIEW

RIGHT OF C.L.

CORRECT APPROACH TRACK

LEFT OF C.L.

Dia 1.10. The ILS beams.

are all aircraft, but this is the shape of things to come. Where airports and aircraft are equipped the limiting factor is not the reliability and safety of the actual landing but the fact that the pilot must have enough visibility after landing to be able to clear the runway and taxi his aircraft to the stand.

How does the aircraft position onto the ILS? We shall be discussing later the method of sequencing aircraft for landing used by ATC. Suffice it to say here that aircraft will be positioned by ATC using radar.

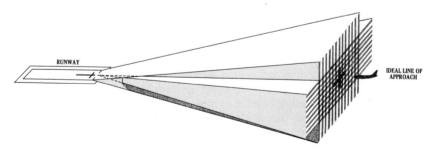

RUNWAY

IDEAL LINE OF APPROACH

Dia 1.11 The ILS segments.

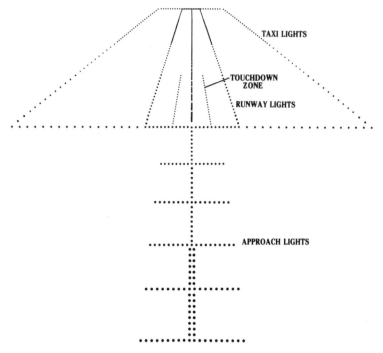

Dia 1.12. Approach and aerodrome lighting.

Airport lighting aids (Dia 1.12)

At night and in poor visibility pilots need some visual assistance in taxiing, taking-off and during the approach and landing. On taxiways and runways this is provided by marking the edges or centre-line, or both, with lights which are blue or green for taxiways and white for runways. In addition there may be different coloured lights to indicate that a pilot may not pass a certain point without ATC permission or to indicate the runway touchdown zone to the pilot of a landing aircraft.

For aircraft approaching to land there is an approach light system consisting of a centre-line of white lights extending for up to 900 m (985 yd) into the approach with up to five white crossbars. The landing pilot may see these lights before he sees the runway lights but they will lead him to the runway.

All these lights are adjustable for intensity, the brighter settings being used in poor visibility and the dimmer for clear dark nights when the lights will stand out well for many miles away.

Chapter 2
Controlled and Special Rules Airspace

Up to and during the Second World War the airspace above the United Kingdom was considered to belong largely to the RAF and other military users. Since there was very little civil flying anyway, there was no case to separate civil and military aircraft. Pilots had to keep their eyes open and hope that others were doing the same.

The great advances in aircraft design and reliability made during the war led to a significant expansion of civil aviation in the post-war years and this continues even now. More modern aircraft began to fly faster and higher and in any weather conditions and the 'see and be seen' concept for avoidance was clearly not good enough, at least for passenger-carrying aircraft.

But what to do? We had neither the equipment, the facilities nor the staff to control all aircraft flying in UK airspace. In any case many pilots did not wish to be under positive control. How could a military exercise be subject to ATC? What about pilot-training, gliders, joy-rides even? Those who really wanted an ATC service and protection from other aircraft were the commercial airline operators and, if ATC was to protect them, it was necessary to segregate them from those categories of aircraft which neither required nor wished for such a service.

We turned to a system which was already in use in the USA and which was being recommended for world-wide use by ICAO: controlled airspace for those who wanted an ATC separation and regulation service and uncontrolled airspace for those who wished to fly without ATC constraints. The first, rather faltering steps were taken in the early 1950s, and the system has been developed and expanded through a process which is still under continuous review by the National Air Traffic Services (NATS) Headquarters, an organisation which is part of the Civil Aviation Authority and which has both civil and military elements.

Why military? Well, both military and civil flying operations need to co-exist and civil and military ATC staffs work jointly to ensure the best use of the available airspace. However, this book is not concerned with military requirements. Their needs are quite different from those of the civil commercial operators whose main concern is that they should fly in a controlled, regulated and highly organized environment so as to ensure the safety of their passengers. In order to provide such an environment, civil and military agreement must be reached on the airspace which can be set aside for commercial use and the means by which military aircraft may occasionally enter this airspace, should they require to do so, while guaranteeing the safety of civil users.

The civil operator requires protection in three areas. While taking off and landing at airports, during the climb to or descent from en route cruising altitudes, and around the routes between airports. The en route protection crosses national boundaries and the other forms of controlled airspace defined in this chapter are also established in other countries. For ATC technical reasons the same type of airspace may be referred to as either 'Controlled Airspace' or 'Special Rules Airspace'. There are very slight differences in the conditions of use but these are not relevant to the airline passenger. Pilots wishing to use any of these categories may do so only with ATC permission (Dia 2.1 and Dia 2.2).

The Control Zone/Special Rules Zone
Controlled airspace established around an airport extends from ground level upwards. It protects aircraft taking off and landing and ensures that all aircraft in the vicinity of an airport are known to controllers who can then provide a safe ATC service. A zone may also include such things as helicopter routes or corridors for access to and from small airfields within the zone but these will always be planned in such a way that aircraft using them will remain clear of traffic using the main airport.

The Control Area/Special Rules Area
An aircraft approaching to land at an airport using ILS for guidance will be descending through about 3000ft at a distance of ten miles from touchdown. An aircraft taking off and climbing away will be at or above 2500ft at the same distance from take-off. At that stage aircraft no longer need protection down to ground level, and so the zone stops about there. But aircraft still need protection and now it is provided from a specified height above the ground (say 2000ft) to take them up to cruising levels. Such airspace is called a Control Area or Special Rules Area and not only does it protect climbing and descending aircraft, it also provides safe airspace for aircraft which are required to await their turns for landing when, for example, the airport is very busy.

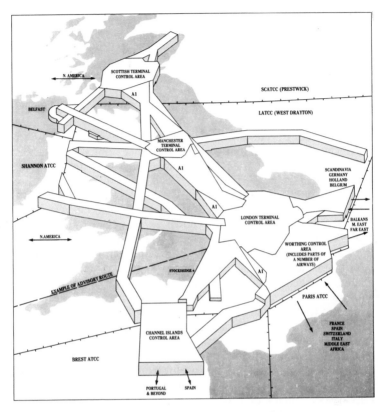

Dia 2.1. UK airways and main control areas.

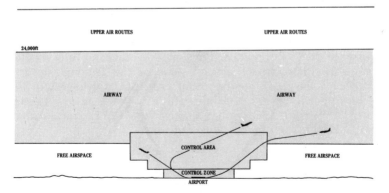

Dia 2.2. Types of controlled and special rules airspace.

The Airway

An Airway is a corridor of controlled airspace protecting an air route, a sort of aerial highway. These corridors are normally ten miles wide and extend from a few thousand feet above ground to 24500ft. In fact they really extend up to 46000ft but they are called Upper Air Routes above 24500ft. Again, aircraft using airways must have ATC permission so that controllers can provide a safe service. And aircraft wishing to cross airways may do so either under the control of the civil airway controller or of an RAF controller working in liaison with the civil controller. Airways cross national boundaries and are identified by a letter/number code, eg, Golf One (G1), Romeo Two Five (R25), Bravo Three (B3). Aircraft follow these routes using VORs and the routes interconnect just as roads do. As an example Airway Alpha One (A1) starts at Glasgow, runs down to Worthing on the south coast, then crosses France, routes to the west of Italy and across the Mediterranean and it can be joined by aircraft at any point or left to join another intersecting airway.

Outside these types of controlled airspace aircraft may fly without ATC permission except, of course, at aerodromes. And pilots are free to choose whether to fly within controlled airspace or outside it. But that is not quite the end of the subject. ATC also notifies a small number of preferred routes outside controlled airspace known as 'Advisory Routes'. These are not busy enough to justify airway status but are useful from time to time and they are published so that all airspace users are aware of them, as are military controllers, etc. A pilot wishing to use such a route will be given an ATC service and a pilot wishing to cross an advisory route can call the controlling authority to ask for details of any activity on it. If and when an advisory route becomes busy enough to justify airway status negotiations are set in hand for possible upgrading.

Looking at Dia 2.1 it appears that there is not very much UK airspace that is not regulated in some way, and this drawing does not show the airspace around some of the regional airports. However, the idea is not to prevent aircraft from flying where they wish to but to ensure that those which fly in the more congested areas are known to controllers and can be given clearances which will make life safer for everyone concerned.

Chapter 3
Control Towers and Air Traffic Control Centres

The Control Tower

There can be few people who would not recognize the control tower at an airport. Everyone knows that the controllers working there are equipped with radio and radar and that their job is to control landings and take-offs and other airport activities. Films and TV often give the impression of barely-controlled panic, constant emergencies, and controllers rushing about tearing their hair and shouting or having nervous breakdowns. ATCOs find all this mildly amusing because they know that it is not like that at all.

Control towers are comparatively quiet places. Each controller has a particular job to do and there is a VHF channel for each one. They wear head-sets with earphones and microphones so that their hands are free to operate the various equipment they use but, of course, the use of earphones reduces the noise level which is no more than it would be when telephones are being used in an office.

Except at very small airports, control towers are divided into two sections, aerodrome control and approach control. Aerodrome controllers work in the glass box (the Visual Control Room) which can be seen on the top of the building because they need to see all the activity on the aerodrome, but approach controllers sequence (direct) aircraft between airways and airports and, since this is invariably done using radar, they work in a separate, darkened room. ATCOs at airports rotate through the various control positions so that they are completely familiar with all the airport ATC procedures.

Aerodrome Control

An aerodrome consists of a runway or runways on which aircraft land and take off, taxiways for access between the runways and parking and maintenance areas, grass areas between and around runways and taxiways, and sites for various installations such as ILS and radar aerials. All these areas come under the authority of ATC and they are known as the manoeuvring area. Parking and maintenance areas are the responsibility of the airport operator.

Any aircraft, vehicle or person wishing to go on to the manoeuvring area must first obtain permission from ATC. There are many reasons for being on the aerodrome, the first and most obvious being for landing and take-off or taxiing to and from the runway, but there are many more. Good housekeeping requires that the concrete or tarmac runways and taxiways are regularly inspected (at least twice a day) and that they are maintained, resurfaced and swept when necessary because odd bits of tarmac or stones could be sucked into jet engines and cause some very expensive damage. Lighting fittings must be regularly checked for unserviceable bulbs or broken glass, painted lines and markings need attention from time to time, grass has to be cut, flocks of birds must be scared off. And then there is radio and radar equipment sited on the aerodrome which has to be serviced regularly.

But even that is not all. An airline may wish to move aircraft between passenger terminals, cargo areas and maintenance hangars and it is more economical to use tractors (called 'tugs') for this purpose than to have to start the aircraft engines and keep pilots waiting around just in case they are needed. So the airport authorities issue their own driving licences and those who need to drive on the aerodrome must pass a test in procedures for and knowledge of that airport and are also trained in the use of RT. Vehicles on aerodromes are controlled in just the same way that aircraft are controlled and ATC will always know which vehicles are on the aerodrome, where they are and why. Just as aircraft have RT callsigns, so do vehicles, eg, 'Sweeper One', 'Works Seven' and 'Speedbird Tug One Five'.

There will be at least two ATCOs in the Visual Control Room, one responsible for landings, take-offs and any other activity on the runway ('−Tower') and the other to control and co-ordinate all other activity on the manoeuvring area ('−Ground'). There may be a third who will be responsible for planning and organization ('−Delivery').

Approach Control
Approach Control (APC) at an airport has a very different function from Aerodrome Control. It provides the link between airways and airports and uses radar to sort and sequence inbound aircraft.

Ideally, aircraft inbound to an airport would arrive in a stream at a single entry point on the final approach to the runway at distances apart which would permit them to continue for a landing without delay, the distances apart being between four and eight miles depending on the particular airport and the types of aircraft. In fact, and particularly in the London area, arrivals are from all directions and may be through up to four different entry points for each airport. Routes to those entry points will be controlled by different en route controllers and APC is necessary to accept arrivals through the different entry points and co-ordinate them into a single, properly spaced stream before transferring them to the tower controller who will in turn co-ordinate landing and departing aircraft.

To achieve an orderly flow of aircraft, both inbound and outbound, airports have scheduling committees made up of all the operators using the airport who decide among themselves the times of landings and take-offs. A free-for-all might see thousands of passengers arriving at the same time to get onto a number of aircraft all due to take off within minutes of each other. This could lead first to congestion on the roads to the airport and in the airport buildings, at customs, etc., and then there would be delays on take-off because a runway can only be used for one take-off at a time and spaces must be left for landing aircraft.

On the arrival side, scheduling is meant to ensure a smooth, uninterrupted flow of aircraft and takes similar account of congestion in airport buildings and roads, etc. However, aircraft are subject to the vagaries of weather, head winds, tail winds, industrial action, problems with late or lost passengers and many other things which will cause them to arrive late or early. So instead of, perhaps, one arrival every three minutes, there could sometimes be ten in ten minutes and this is more than the runway can cope with.

The answer is to delay some of the aircraft at the entry points and then to sequence them at the required intervals. The procedure is this. The entry point is actually known as the holding point and the control of airspace there is shared by en route sector controllers and the approach controllers. The en route controllers will clear the first arrival to the holding point at 7000ft, the second at 8000ft and so on at intervals of 1000ft and will telephone the approach controller to tell him the arrival order and altitudes of the aircraft. There may be a number of en route controllers doing this at the same time but to different holding points.

The approach controllers, using radar, see the aircraft approaching the holding points and decide whether they can be directed into the approach sequence or whether they should be delayed (held) at the holding points, When RT control is transferred from en route (ie. when aircraft are at their different cleared altitudes) to approach control they will instruct pilots accordingly.

From this stage APC will either hold aircraft or sequence them from the bottom of the 'holding stack' and then clear them for further descent to begin the approach for landing. As the lower altitudes are vacated, higher aircraft are cleared down into them and further en route arrivals are fed onto the top of the stack (Dia 3.1).

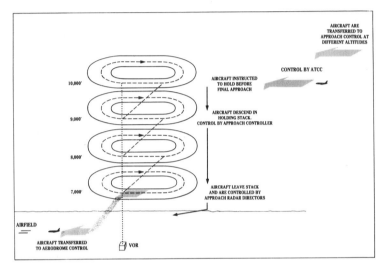

Dia 3.1. A holding pattern.

What happens when aircraft are instructed to hold is that they fly to the holding point (usually a VOR) and then turn to the opposite direction (outbound) for one minute, then turn again to fly back to the holding point, repeating the procedure as necessary. There can be a number of aircraft doing this at the same time but all at different altitudes (that is why it is called a holding stack). So the en route controllers feed the stack at the top with aircraft at different altitudes and then transfer them to approach control. The approach controllers will decide on the intervals of time or distance apart to take them out of the stack from the bottom and may be co-ordinating arrivals through up to four stacks. They will then direct those aircraft into a single stream at the required distances apart and guide them onto the final approach at a point from which they can continue the approach using ILS and land. APC will already have advised the tower of the landing order and when aircraft are settled on the ILS they will be transferred to the tower for landing clearance.

This is not a one-man operation and, in fact, there are normally three ATCOs involved. The Approach Controller provides the links with en route and tower controllers and instructs aircraft to descend in the stack(s). The No 1 Radar Director makes the decisions on when and how aircraft leave the stack and begins the initial approach sequence; he then transfers control to the No 2 Radar Director who will make the finer adjustments necessary to ensure the proper spacing for landing.

The Air Traffic Control Centre
A control tower must, of course, be at an airport but an Air Traffic Control Centre (ATCC) can be anywhere and the ATCC which controls all the airways and routes over England, Wales and Northern Ireland is at West Drayton, about two miles north of Heathrow.

The ATCCs are much bigger and more complex organizations than control towers and there are about five times as many operational ATCOs at the London ATCC at West Drayton than there are in the control tower at Heathrow Airport. An ATCC will also have a much bigger supporting staff than a control tower.

The UK has two ATCCs, London ATCC (LATCC — spoken as 'Latsea') and Scottish ATCC (Sc ATCC) at Prestwick. Around them are ATCCs at Stavanger, Copenhagen, Amsterdam, Brussels, Paris, Brest and Shannon and beyond them are other ATCCs responsible for the airspace above every continent and all the oceans of the world (Dia 3.2). All use standard ICAO procedures, the English language and even Greenwich Mean Time so as to avoid confusion in the transfer of aircraft from one ATCC to another.

All ATCCs have the same function which is to control those Airways, Control Areas and routes which are not the immediate concern of airports. So an aircraft taking off from Heathrow to Birmingham would be transferred to LATCC control after take-off and remain under their control until being transferred to Birmingham APC. An aircraft from Gatwick to Paris would, again, be transferred to LATCC after take-off but would then be passed on to Paris ATCC who would transfer it to De Gaulle, Orly or Le Bourget APC. Similarly aircraft from or over-flying the Paris area inbound to the London area would be transferred from Paris ATCC to LATCC where the sector controllers would separate them from aircraft over-flying the London area, descend them to stack levels and then transfer them to APC at the destination airport (Dia 3.3). Some aircraft, eg, from the USA to Europe, neither land nor take off in the UK and such an 'overflight' would enter LATCC airspace from Shannon, be

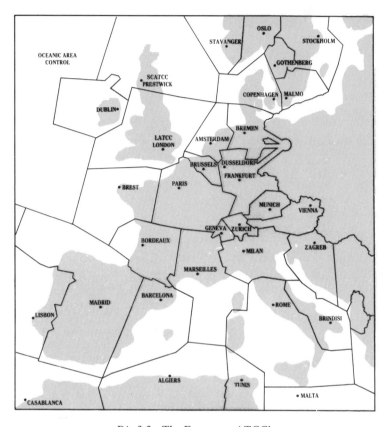

Dia 3.2. The European ATCC's.

controlled by LATCC controllers and then be transferred to Brussels ATCC for onward clearance in the standard way.

Within LATCC, because the airspace is much too vast to be controlled in one operation, ATCOs operate sectors. The London Area (known as the London Terminal Control Area — LTMA) is divided into four separate sectors and spoke-like around the LTMA are the Daventry and Pole Hill sectors to the north, Clacton to the east, Bristol to the west and the Hurn, Seaford, Lydd and Dover sectors to the south. ATCOs will usually be qualified in three or four sectors so that they do not become too parochial.

About an hour before a flight becomes active in UK airspace, all sectors which will handle the aircraft will receive advance notification. When the flight enters UK airspace, either off the ground at an airport or via another ATCC, this information becomes 'live' and is displayed at all relevant control positions. Ten minutes before an aircraft is due to leave one sector for another the flight is co-ordinated and control is transferred at or before the sector boundary. When an aircraft is crossing from one ATCC's area to another the same procedure applies.

The sector controllers are supported by a number of other people (more of that later) but their job is to concentrate on the radar, to climb departing aircraft to their cruising levels, to descend inbound aircraft to levels at which they can be transferred to APC and to integrate overflights. Aircraft within five miles of each other must be separated vertically by at least 1000ft. Some sectors operate in one direction only, others in two directions and these latter are further divided into two sub-sectors.

This chapter has outlined the way in which the ATC service is organized. It has shown the areas and divisions of responsibility which need to be understood before we look at the various units in detail, and that we shall be doing later. We can see what happens to the aircraft from the time the passenger boards it and the doors are closed until it leaves UK airspace, as well as the procedures for arriving flights. The systems in other countries are much the same and passengers may be assured that their safety is the first consideration of any ATC service.

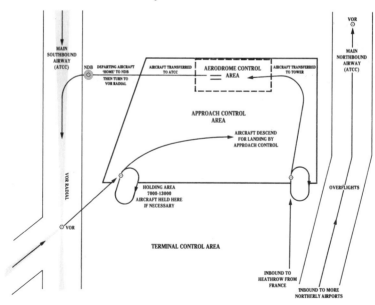

Dia 3.3. Areas controlled by ATCC, APC and aerodrome control.

Chapter 4
The Development of Airports

The pioneers of aviation would be surprised, I think, to see a modern airport. In their day an airfield was just a flat field and, if your field was not big enough, all you had to do was to flatten a hedge or fill in a ditch, build a shed or two for garaging or servicing, and you were in business. The advantage of a big field was that aircraft could land or take off in any direction and it was important to operate into wind so that there was no sideways stress on the wheels (called undercarts or undercarriages) from crosswinds. The disadvantage of a grass landing area was that, as aircraft became heavier, they tended to sink into the mud during wet weather.

In the UK the RAF took the lead in the development of runway aerodromes. During the build-up before the Second World War when both bomber aircraft and their bomb loads were becoming heavier it was important that operations should not be restricted because of waterlogged airfields and the concept of the three-runway aerodrome was developed. The main (longest) runway was always into the prevailing wind, which is from the south-west, and two subsidiary runways intersected the main runway at angles of about 60° (Dia 4.1). Since each runway has two ends, this meant that there was a choice of six landing/take-off directions and aircraft could still land and take off reasonably into wind. By 1939 many RAF aerodromes also had Standard Beam Approach installed on main runways as well as aerodrome and approach lighting systems.

During the war years there were not too many advances in ATC. Radar was developed for ATC use following its earlier requirement to see and intercept enemy aircraft and there were some improvements in approach and landing aids but, when Heathrow was taken over during the early post-war years to be developed as Britain's major civil airport, it was based on the RAF's three-runway concept. The great difference was that each runway was then duplicated by a second, parallel runway and Heathrow, therefore, was able to operate in any of six directions and, in each direction, it could have landings on one runway and take-offs on a parallel runway. Alternatively, if a runway was blocked or required maintenance, the parallel runway was

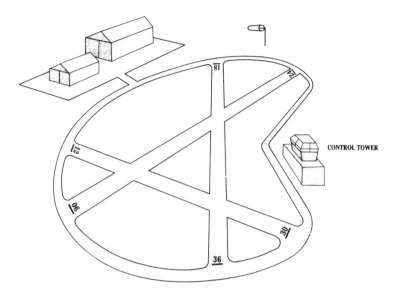

CONTROL TOWER

Dia 4.1. A typical three-runway aerodrome.

available. All the passenger facilities were developed at the centre of this runway complex and access was via a tunnel under one of the main runways.

It seemed a good idea at the time but it is unlikely that it would be designed in the same way today. For a start, in 1945, no-one could have envisaged the enormous growth in the air transport industry, the number of airlines requiring facilities, the millions of passengers or even the need for so many car parks. As a result, it has been necessary to extend the central area to such an extent that three of the original six runways have been built over. But, owing to advances in aircraft design the closed runways were no longer required, anyway, since crosswinds are not as critical as they used to be.

Heathrow is the only airport ever built in the UK with parallel runways. Others, such as Gatwick and Luton, have been developed as single-runway airports with facilities and access to one side of the runway. However, the need for more space is common to them all, but space is simply not available at the present locations so Stansted is to be enlarged and modernized.

Most of our airports started their lives as RAF or RN airfields and it was never too big a problem to convert them for civil use. The manoeuvring areas were certainly up to the required standard but some of the buildings such as barrack blocks were unsuitable and a certain amount of rebuilding has taken place. Military establishments by their very nature tend to be rather drab so where they have been taken over they have been prettied up to make them more welcoming to the public.

Over the years there has been a lot of talk about developing 'green field sites' or even constructing an airport out to sea off the east coast but both the costs and the problems would be so enormous that it seems hardly likely. In fact the whole subject has been rather a hot potato and the hope is that regional airports, most of which are under-utilized, will begin to play a greater role in meeting the demands of the airline industry. There must be a lot of people who hope so.

Chapter 5
Numbering of Runways and Direction of Operations

Runways are laid down as near as possible into the prevailing wind which is usually between southwest and west in the UK, and such things as built-up areas, hills and radio masts must also be taken into account in the alignment.

The reasons why aircraft should land and take off into wind are, first, so that there is the minimum sideways wind force on the aircraft, particularly when it touches down, and, second, if an aeroplane must maintain an airspeed (speed through the air) of 120 knots to enable it to fly then, if it can land or take off into a 20 knot wind, its ground speed (in this case the speed of the wheels on the ground) will be only 100 knots (Dia 5.1). So, the approach and landing are easier into wind and the lower wheel speeds are good for the tyres and brakes.

Runways are numbered according to their direction. We know that a compass indicates direction in degrees from north and any direction can be expressed this way. So we measure the direction of a runway (always in three figures from 001° to 360°), take it to the nearest 10° and use the first two figures as the runway number, eg, direction 274° becomes 270° = runway 27. The other end of the runway is, therefore 094° = 090° = runway 09 (Dia 5.2). In the case of parallel runways one will be referred to as left (L) and the other right (R). Heathrow's parallel runways are 09L/09R and 27L/27R.

Obviously the wind varies from time to time and can be as much as 90° to the runway but the direction of landing and take-off will be that which is most nearly into wind. For most of the time Heathrow will use runways 27L/27R for landing and take-off (this is known as westerly operations) but for about thirty per cent of the year the wind blows from the east and Heathrow will use runways 09L/09R (easterly operations). Similarly, the other airports will operate in easterly or westerly directions as required.

At all UK airports other than Heathrow, landings and take-offs are on a single runway. When Heathrow is using 27L/27R the landing and take-off runways will be alternated at 3 pm each day (unless there is a problem) so as to spread the noise as evenly as possible. People living under the approaches and close to the airport under the departure routes are, therefore, given some measure of relief from noise and, of course, the wear and tear on the runway surfaces is evened out.

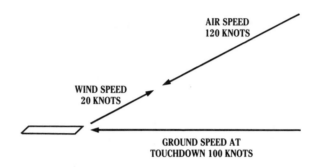

Dia 5.1. The effect of wind on runway speed.

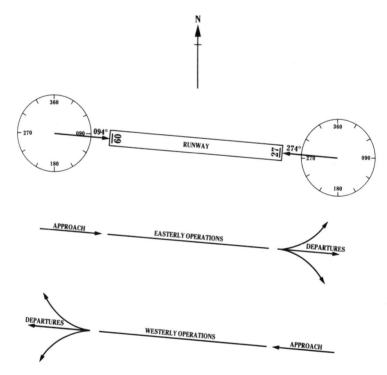

Dia 5.2. Numbering of runways direction of operations.

Part 2

Now that we have some background we can look at the practical application of ATC at airports and Air Traffic Control Centres. In Part 2 we have London's main airports as well as the London ATCC at West Drayton with particular emphasis on its southern area of operations (LATCC South Bank). Also included are chapters on Flow Control, aircraft noise and flights across the North Atlantic. These subjects slot in here because of their general interest but they are equally relevant to Midlands, Northern and Scottish airports which are dealt with in Parts 3 and 4.

Chapter 6
ATC at Heathrow Airport

Heathrow is the world's major international airport. It is used by aircraft from every country in Europe and from every continent in the world as well as by domestic (internal) flights from all over the United Kingdom, a total of more than seventy airlines.

It began its civil life with a few huts and tents on the north side of the airport alongside the Bath road with a tiny control tower nearby. The first permanent facilities were then built in the central area for the passenger-carrying operations with a new control tower (Dia 6.1) commanding a view far beyond the

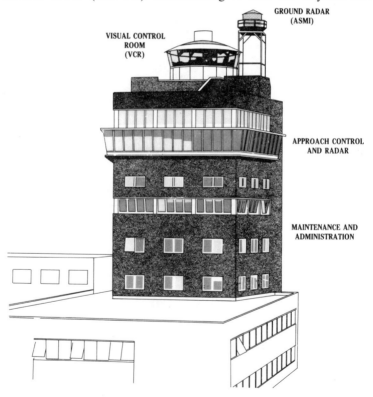

GROUND RADAR
(ASMI)

VISUAL CONTROL
ROOM
(VCR)

APPROACH CONTROL
AND RADAR

MAINTENANCE AND
ADMINISTRATION

Dia 6.1. Control tower at Heathrow.

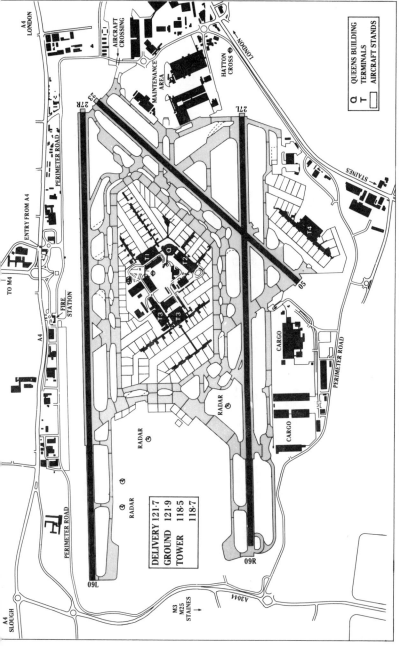

Dia 6.2. Plan of London/Heathrow Airport.

boundaries of the airport. And Heathrow has continued to develop into its present enormous complex with its own links into London's underground and bus route systems. Books have been written about it all but we are concerned here with Air Traffic Control and we can begin by looking at a plan of the airport in Dia 6.2.

Let us examine the runways first; there are three of them. The two major runways lie in an east to west direction, they are parallel and they are over two miles long. They are equipped with the last word in ILS and the most modern lighting systems and are strong enough to take the strain of a jumbo jet touching down at well over 100 mph. One runway is used for take-off and the parallel runway for landings and the choice of direction obviously depends on the surface wind. The subsidiary runway, 05/23, is about 1½ miles long, and is used only occasionally when one of the main runways is out of action for maintenance or when pilots may prefer to use it during strong wind conditions. On all runways certain of the medium and smaller aircraft may elect to take off from an intersection to reduce taxiing distance.

Between the runways and the central terminal area there is a system of taxiways which was originally an inner circular taxiway with access to and from parking areas and an outer circular taxiway with connections to and from the runways. Thus inbound aircraft would route through to the inner taxiway and thence to the parking stands while outbounds joined the outer taxiway en-route to the take-off points. This concept remains but extensions of the terminal area to the west have gone beyond the original taxiways and the system there is not as clearly defined as it was.

Incidentally, because of the vastness of the runway and taxiway areas, they are divided into numbered blocks for the purpose of identification and as you taxi round the airport you may see the block number boards as you move from one block to another. For ATC these numbers can be used to specify a route or a turning point or to identify an area which needs to be closed for such things as surface repairs or sweeping.

The central area has seen many changes over the years. As the terminals were built aircraft parked around the area on numbered stands and passengers disemplaned and walked into the buildings. When the parking areas were extended buses were used, partly to save the passengers' legs and protect them from the weather but also to stop them wandering about and getting in the way. Increasing numbers of both aircraft and passengers led to a demand for improved facilities and a method of getting passengers to and from their aircraft without the need for groups being

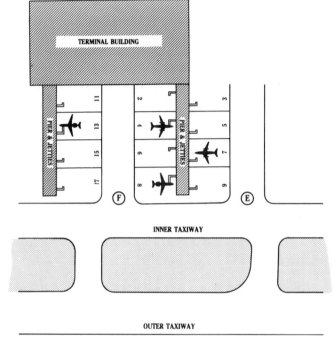

Dia 6.3. Typical cul-de-sac at Heathrow.

led around by airline staff or for buses on the parking areas.

The advent of piers with walkways and jetties between the terminals and the aircraft stands took care of some of the problems and for many stands piers radiate from the terminals to form cul-de-sacs in which aircraft park 'nose-in' to load or off-load their passengers via jetties connected to the piers (Dia 6.3). Passengers can then walk under cover (and out of harm's way) to and from the terminals.

However, traffic has continued to increase and some of the newer stands still require access by coach. But even that extension of the central area has not been enough to cope with further expected increases and Terminal 4 had to be built on the south side of the airport adjacent to the cargo area.

As for the ATC function within this complex, we know that the manoeuvring area is controlled by ATCOs who look out over the aerodrome from the glass box on top of the control tower which is known as the Visual Control Room (VCR). There are four of these controllers at Heathrow: the Ground Movement Planner (GMP), the Ground Movement Controller (GMC), the Air

Controller (Departures) (Air D) and the Air Controller (Arrivals) (Air A).

Each controller is responsible for a particular part of the operation and will accept or transfer control of aircraft as required and the sequence for departure is GMP, GMC and Air (D). Immediately after take-off (except in the case of westerly departures during easterly operations) departing aircraft are transferred to the control of the appropriate TMA sector at LATCC.

Control of arriving aircraft is accepted from LATCC by approach control and sequenced through the arrival points and onto the final approach where they are transferred to Air (A) at about ten miles from touchdown and then to GMC when they have have landed and left the runway.

That is the general idea but, to understand precisely who is responsible for what, we need to look at the divisions in more detail.

Planning the departures
In-depth departure planning starts with the Airport Scheduling Committee. They have been told by the BAA that the airport can handle a certain number of departures per hour and the various airlines have made their bids for and been allocated times for their services. The airlines then file flight plans giving details of flight number, aircraft type, time of departure, route, airspeed and destination. One hour before the scheduled departure this information is automatically passed by teleprinter to the tower and is presented to GMP on cardboard flight progress strips (FPS) which are slipped into plastic holders and placed on the pending departures board. GMP can look at this display and can always assess the likely outbound traffic situation for about an hour ahead. Inbound aircraft are similarly notified to Air (A) (Dia 6.4).

The airlines load their aircraft as near to scheduled times as possible and when the pilot is ready to start engines he will call GMP on RT and request permission to start engines. Before giving permission GMP must consider three possibilities. First, how many aircraft are already started and taxiing for take-off, since the departure runway will take an average of one aircraft every ninety seconds (forty per hour) and to have twenty aircraft waiting at the runway for take-off would mean a thirty minute wait for some, and this would waste an enormous amount of very expensive fuel. The ideal is four to six aircraft preferably using different departure routes, and when more aircraft than this are requesting start it is more economical to keep them on the stands

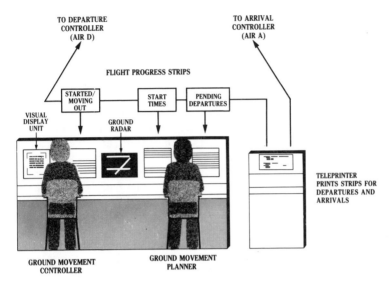

Dia 6.4. Ground planning and movement control.

with engines switched off and to allocate sequenced start times to ensure an even flow of outbound traffic. You might ask what happened to scheduling but remember that such things as bad weather can lead to late arrivals and a consequent build-up for departures.

Second, how many aircraft are already started or are wishing to start for a particular route. Having a number of aircraft arriving at the runway at the same time for the same route would, again, lead to delays because the time interval between departures for the same route is a minimum of two minutes. This may be another reason for start times to be issued.

The third factor for GMP to consider is that routes may be subject to delay or regulation for any of a number of reasons. Aircraft subject to such 'Flow Control' are allocated 'slots' by LATCC and aircraft must be given start-up times to enable them to take off on time (See Chapter 11).

You can see that the GMP really does have to be a planner. He must consider GMC and his workload, Air (D) and the number of aircraft he may have to sort out as well as delays and restrictions imposed by other agencies and circumstances so as to get the operation off to a smooth start, and at the right pace so as not to create unnecessary delays of his own. It can all be quite a headache.

Ground Control

When GMP has done his bit he passes the FPS to GMC (Dia 6.4) who can now look ahead for a limited time. He will be controlling previous departing aircraft as well as aircraft leaving the runway for parking stands and, probably, aircraft being towed to and from maintenance areas, BAA vehicles going about their business of servicing the airport or telecommunications vehicles on their way to and from radar and ILS installations, and it is also very helpful to be able to anticipate which aircraft are likely to call during the next few minutes. This is a job that calls for a very quick and tidy mind and an unflappable disposition.

GMC is a very complex operation. Looking back to Dia 6.2 we can see that much of the traffic is parked in cul-de-sacs although in some areas the stands are adjacent to taxiways. In the latter case the pilot will call GMC for permission to push-back when he has started engines and GMC will give permission to push onto the taxiway when it is clear and no moving aircraft will be obstructed. The pilot will then advise the tug driver on the intercom which is connected between the tug and the aircraft and when push-back is complete the tug will disconnect and move clear. The pilot will then request taxi clearance and be cleared to the runway in use.

Cul-de-sac operation is rather more complicated and we can see this in Dia 6.5. Let us say that BAW 323 has left the runway and has been allocated stand C8, EIN 142 has started engines and, although GMC will know this because he has the FPS on his

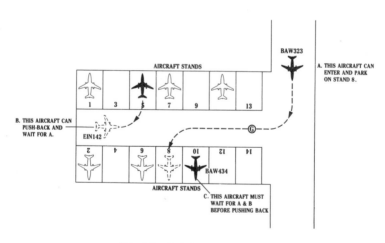

Dia 6.5. Cul-de-sac operation.

display, he does not know when the pilot will call for push-back and may not even know which stand 142 is on.

GMC continues to direct other aircraft to and from the runways and, perhaps, tugs towing aircraft between the stands and the maintenance area, gives permission for a sweeper vehicle to sweep a part of the taxiway and clears an aircraft to push-back onto a taxiway. And then the expected call, 'Heathrow Ground this is Shamrock 142, stand C5, permission to push-back'.

GMC doesn't have time to think about this. He knows the airport like the back of his hand and barely needs to consider that 142 can push-back and will be clear of BAW 323's route to stand C8. 'Shamrock 142 push-back and hold. One aircraft inbound to stand C8.' And then immediately, 'London Ground this is Speedbird 434 stand C10 permission to push-back'. No chance. 'Speedbird 434 standby I will call you'.

And so on. Remember that the main runways are over two miles long and that aircraft taxi quite slowly. GMC can have aircraft under control for up to about fifteen minutes and a lot of aircraft can leave the runway or the stands or ask to push-back during that time. Obviously this is the main task but add it to all the other airport activities which must go on and this might just give an idea of the workload involved.

In daylight and good visibility GMC does all this by looking out, making a continuous assessment of the traffic situation and issuing instructions to all the aircraft, vehicles and working parties under his control. If the weather is misty and the visibility is reduced GMC uses a radar called the Air to Surface Movement Indicator (ASMI) which looks down on the airport from a few feet above the VCR.

At night things look quite different and everyone involved, GMC, pilots, drivers, needs a bit of help. Out on the dark aerodrome it would be too easy not to see the lights of an aircraft or vehicle against the mass of lights in the central area and the pilot would find it impossible to taxi around without some help. That help is provided by a person known as the lighting operator or 'GMC's best friend'.

Heathrow has a very advanced airport lighting system which is controlled from a panel in the VCR. The approach lights are straightforward enough (Dia 1.11) and it is usually a case of selecting whichever lights are required and adjusting the intensity for the conditions.

The taxiway lighting system is quite fascinating. All taxiways and cul-de-sacs have green centre-line lights and wherever routes cross there is a bar of red lights either side of the

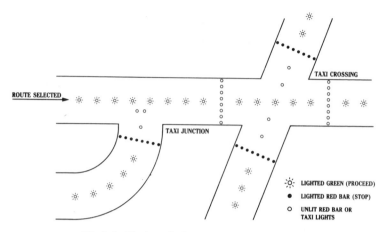

Dia 6.6. Taxiway lights at London/Heathrow.

intersection on both routes (Dia 6.6). If a route is selected across an intersection or a junction any lights crossing or joining the route are automatically extinguished and red stop bars appear to protect the selected route. Thus only one route can go through and all crossing or joining traffic is stopped.

The lighting operator listens in to the GMC frequency and selects routes according to the instructions issued. He is another pair of eyes for GMC. He has a detailed knowledge of the manoeuvring area and provides a constantly changing pattern of green routes and red bars around the airport. It is hard work but life without him would be very difficult.

By day or night when an arriving aircraft is on the stand it switches off the engines and is of no further concern to GMC. A departing aircraft is different in that Air (D) will want to know about it as soon as possible so that he can fit it into his sequence and so, when GMC has instructed the departure to a point where it has a clear, unobstructed route to the runway, he will pass the FPS to, and instruct the pilot to call, the Air Controller (D).

The control of take-offs (Dia 6.7)
Air (D) has a pretty good idea of what GMC is sending his way but his first positive indication is when he receives the FPS and by the time this arrives it may contain rather more information than it started with. It will show the time at which engine start was requested and the time allocated if this was different, the departure route into the LTMA (we can look at that when we

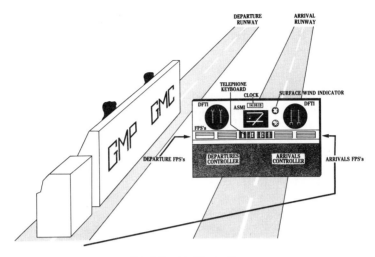

Dia 6.7. Air Controllers.

discuss the TMA) and the slot time if there is one, as well as any special information given to that aircraft. The FPS has become a little history of the flight so far.

Air (D) takes the strip and looks at two things. Is there a slot time and which way will the aircraft turn after take-off? If there is

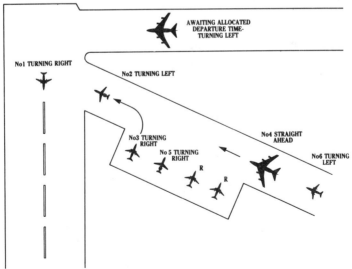

Dia 6.8. Arranging the stream at the holding point.

no slot time then it can be fitted into the departure sequence quite simply but if there is a slot time it must be fitted in at a particular point. Some aircraft may be cleared to enter the runway for take-off immediately, those that have to wait do so at what is called the Holding Point.

What Air (D) aims to do as departing aircraft are transferred to his control is to set up a pattern of aircraft which will be turning in alternating directions after take-off. They will either turn left or right or fly more or less straight ahead to follow the initial departure routes through the TMA and they are 'juggled' at the holding point to form the pattern (Dia 6.8).

There is a very good reason for this. The minimum time interval between departures using the same routes is two minutes but when a following aircraft turns a different way the minimum interval is reduced to one minute, so the departure rate is increased by using the left, right, straight ahead technique. But there is a little more to it than that. Aircraft are grouped according to size and speed and when an aircraft from a faster group follows a slower one, extra time must be added. Similarly when an aircraft from any other group follows a jumbo the minimum interval is two minutes regardless of the direction of turn. There is a lot of mental arithmetic involved, particularly when aircraft with slot times have to be fitted in and the controller must make the most efficient use of his runway because scheduling is based on that.

When the aircraft is airborne Air (D) has finished his part of the operation and at about the time it is crossing the end of the runway he will call 'Speedbird 162 was airborne at time 1615, contact London Control frequency 128.4'. The time is fed into the computer, this triggers off FPSs at all the required positions at LATCC and the aircraft comes under the control of the London TMA controller.

Air (D) does not entirely forget the aircraft, however. On his desk is a small radar screen which is called a Distance From Touchdown Indicator (DFTI) but in this case is used in reverse to show departing aircraft. Air (D) watches the aircraft as it climbs away just to make sure that everything is as it should be during those few seconds of transfer of control.

So, you see, there is always somebody watching the progress of your aircraft and that is part of the ATC contribution toward making this a very safe transport system.

The approach and landing

We shall look at approach control and radar later; it is enough to say here that they are the link between en route control and the aerodrome controllers and that they will organize aircraft into a single stream at the correct intervals for landing and position them onto the ILS for the final approach to the runway.

In the tower, Air (A) will have received advance information on arriving aircraft from the teleprinter on FPSs. Later the approach radar director advises him of the actual order of arrival and he will arrange his strips in sequence. If there is anything Air (A) should be reminded of, such as a sick passenger whose aircraft will require expeditious handling, this will be done, too.

Air (A) will then know which aircraft is which as they appear on his DFTI and when they call him on transfer of control from approach. He will then be responsible for seeing that the proper spacing is maintained to touchdown.

This controller must ensure that pilots are aware of the state of the runway surface if it is other than dry, and the direction and speed of the surface wind. They must be informed of any problem such as a closed turn-off, work in progress near the runway and anything else which is the least bit unusual.

It is his responsibility to decide when it is safe to clear an aircraft to land and if it is not, he must instruct it to overshoot. If that happens, Air (A) must first tell Air (D) so that departing aircraft and the overshoot can be kept clear of each other. As an example, the overshoot could be instructed to climb straight ahead to 1000ft and a departing aircraft from the parallel runway straight ahead to 2000ft before turning. A following departure might then be delayed until the overshoot is clear of its route. Air (A) must then co-ordinate a procedure with approach radar control to resequence the aircraft back into the landing sequence.

A word about overshoots. They will be initiated by Air (A) if he considers that an aircraft should not land for any reason or by the pilot if he has the slightest doubt about the runway, the wind, his own aircraft, an aircraft ahead being slow to clear the runway or any of a host of reasons. An overshoot is a perfectly safe and normal procedure and is certainly nothing to be alarmed about. It is all about maintaining the safety standard; the problem is that it will probably take ten minutes or more to go round the circuit and get back to the landing runway so it really boils down to being a nuisance, but no more.

To put all this together, in busy periods up to 75 aircraft can use Heathrow for take-off and landing in one hour. In addition there will be aircraft being towed between parking stands and maintenance areas, some of which will need to cross runways and must, therefore, be fitted in between departing or arriving

44

aircraft, as well as vehicles engaged in various activities which must be allowed to continue. Working parties must be given the facility to re-surface where required, to change light fittings, to sweep. Runways must be inspected and sometimes closed for a period, in which case runway 05/23 might be brought into use or the whole operation carried out on one runway.

Although each controller is responsible for his or her own part of the operation they are very much a team whose dedication and acceptance of responsibility will ensure the safety and efficiency of Heathrow Airport.

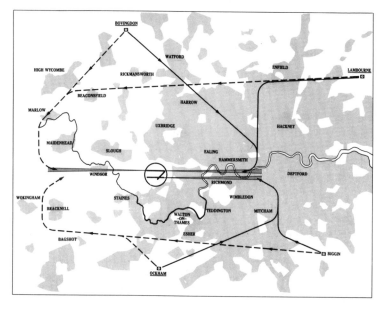

Dia 6.9. Location of the entry points.
Approach routes for Easterly _ _ _ _ and Westerly _____ operations (approximate).

Approach control and radar

Meanwhile, down on the 6th floor another team of ATCOs is carrying out an entirely different function. There are five controllers here, they work in near darkness and the only light is provided by illuminated FPS displays and the amber glow from radar screens. The atmosphere is quiet, almost peaceful, any noise being absorbed by carpets and acoustic tiling, etc. This is Approach Control.

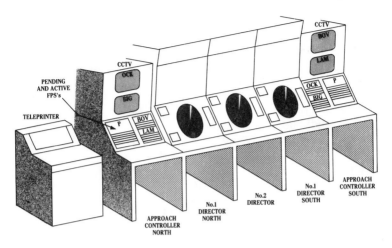

6.10. Heathrow approach control.

We discussed approach control in general in Chapter 3. Heathrow has its control zone extending up to 2500ft but the entry points lie outside the zone in the LTMA. Each entry point has VOR/DME and there are two to the north of the airport named Bovingdon and Lambourne and two to the south named Ockham and Biggin (Dia 6.9). The arrival routes are aligned on these VORs and transfer of control to Heathrow takes place at the VORs.

To control four of these arrival points would be too much for one control position so approach control is divided into two sectors, north handling traffic via Bovingdon and Lambourne and south controlling the arrivals through Ockham and Biggin. For each of these sectors there are two controllers (Dia 6.10). One is known as the Approach Controller; he sits in front of an FPS display and his first job is to liaise with LATCC to accept notification of impending arrivals at each of his two entry points, their time of arrival and the level to which they have been cleared. The holding levels are from 7000ft to 13000ft and we already know that aircraft are cleared in by en route control at different levels starting at the bottom of the stack; the Approach Controller provides a double check that aircraft are at their correct separated levels.

Having received the notification, he writes the time and level on the FPS which has already been printed out by the teleprinter and puts the strip(s) in his display under the appropriate VOR designator. This display is televised and can be seen both by the en route controllers who are handing over the traffic and at the opposite approach control position; if aircraft are instructed to hold at the VOR a big 'H' is written on the strip and when aircraft are descended in the stack, levels are crossed off as they are vacated. In this way the opposite approach sector can see what is going on and the en route controllers know what levels are available to them.

The other controller in each sector team is the Number One Director (North or South) and he sits alongside the Approach Controller in front of a radar screen. He doesn't talk to LATCC direct but he watches very closely the FPS display and relates that information to what he sees on his radar and, again, he ensures that aircraft are at the correct level on transfer of control. He also watches the other sector's televised FPS display because he must know about all inbound traffic.

So we have two teams (North and South) controlling their own sector and watching the other, but so far the aircraft have only reached the holding points. This is where the No 1 Directors take over. Each one will know what aircraft are inbound to all four VORs and it is their job to bring aircraft on into the landing stream, to have the right number of aircraft in that stream or to put aircraft into the holding pattern when that number will be exceeded.

On a good day when everything is on schedule or when the traffic is light it may be possible to clear all arrivals to leave the VORs to join the landing stream. When there are too many aircraft then at some stage they will be instructed to join the holding pattern. This is what the pilot means when he tells his passengers 'We shall arrive at Heathrow on time subject to any ATC delays' but I should point out that ATC are not causing the delays, they are merely responding to an overload situation in the safest possible way, no matter how inconvenient and irritating the delay may be.

If aircraft are instructed to hold, the time of entry is noted on the strip and they are brought on in the order of their arrival at the VORs. The trick now is to convert the vertical arrival and stack system into a stream of aircraft descending into the zone and to position them onto the final approach on the ILS at the right intervals for landing.

How do they decide? Well, there are no computers or other devices to do it for them. There never have been and there will not be for the foreseeable future. They operate on a basis of training, practice and experience. It takes several months to learn

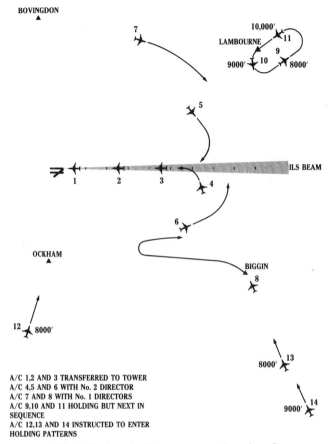

BOVINGDON

7

10,000'
LAMBOURNE   11
9
9000'   10   8000'

5

ILS BEAM
1   2   3   4

6

OCKHAM

BIGGIN
8

12   8000'

13
8000'

14
9000'

A/C 1,2 AND 3 TRANSFERRED TO TOWER
A/C 4,5 AND 6 WITH No. 2 DIRECTOR
A/C 7 AND 8 WITH No. 1 DIRECTORS
A/C 9,10 AND 11 HOLDING BUT NEXT IN
SEQUENCE
A/C 12,13 AND 14 INSTRUCTED TO ENTER
HOLDING PATTERNS

Dia 6.11. A typical busy sequence (numbered).

how to do this but, with practice, controllers learn to assess a continuously changing situation by watching the radar as well as the FPSs for four VORs.

It may be that all the traffic is arriving through one sector for a while and the No 1 is concerned only with the integration of traffic from his own two holding points. When aircraft are arriving through all four VORs the two No 1s will talk to each other on an intercom and agree a sequence (Dia 6.11). In fact experienced controllers can almost read each other's minds and may simply number the strips in sequence and bring them off without a word being necessary. ATCOs do not make unnecessary phone calls because they can be a distraction.

That description may be an over-simplification. Remember that if aircraft from one side of the final approach have a tailwind, aircraft from the other sector will have a headwind and this could make a great difference to their speed over the ground which is also their speed across the radar screen. Aircraft holding may be at the VOR or at the other end of the holding pattern which can be six miles away so the procedure is not being started from fixed points. Different types of aircraft will fly at different speeds so a catching up or falling back element must be included in the calculation.

Whatever, once the No 1 has directed aircraft clear of the holding point he will clear them to descend from stack levels to about 3000ft. This will leave a space at the bottom of the stack and holding aircraft can be cleared by the Approach Controller to descend to lower levels. As each level is vacated the next aircraft above can descend to fill the vacated level and this can all be seen by the LATCC controller who will feed subsequent arrivals to the top of the stack before transferring them to approach control.

The No 1s have enough to do watching, calculating, co-ordinating and directing aircraft into the sequence and when the initial stream is set up on the right headings and speeds and in the descent clear of the stack, they will transfer control to the No 2 Director who sits between them.

The No 2 has, in effect, a third sector which encompasses the final approach. He will accept aircraft from the north or south, adjust the headings and speeds if necessary, and turn them onto the final approach at intervals which will depend upon the aircraft type. If a following aircraft is from the same group, that will be four miles but if a jumbo is followed by an aircraft from a medium group it will be six miles. When a light aircraft follows a jumbo the interval is eight miles but a light following a medium may require six miles and when a slow aircraft is followed by a fast the No 2 must calculate a distance behind the slow aircraft so that when it touches down the faster aircraft will be four miles behind it. If the runway surface is very wet or icy these distances may have to be increased. This is not easy and requires a lot of practice and experience to get it right, but it *must* be right. No 2 knows that he will be unpopular with Air (A) if he gets aircraft too close because it could result in an overshoot and if he gets them too far apart the whole system is slowed down and more aircraft will have to hold for longer. It is the No 2 who advises the tower of the landing order and when aircraft are settled onto the ILS he will transfer them to Air (A) for the final approach and the landing clearance.

And so to the landing, transfer to GMC and on to the stand.

When the aircraft is ready to depart he will call GMP, and so on ad infinitum. Aircraft come and go 365 days a year, controllers change shifts three times a day and may work in any control position because it is important that they are familiar with all aspects of the system. And all in the interests of safety first with as much expedition as possible for the maintenance of schedules and the convenience of passengers.

Flight in the later stages

It is not, strictly speaking, a function of a book about ATC to talk about aircraft performance. However, there are phases of flight during which there are changes which seem to disturb some passengers and it might be reassuring for some to know about them.

An aircraft needs most power to climb, less to cruise and low power to descend. Some have passenger cabin altimeters so that passengers can associate a reduction of power with levelling off at cruising altitude or with the beginning of the descent. When they do not have such indicators the power reductions are fairly obvious.

Jet aircraft at high levels fly above most of the weather and may experience just the odd bump but as they descend into weather at lower levels the air can become unstable, giving rise to quite bouncy conditions. Nothing to worry about; aircraft are built to stand much rougher weather than they are ever likely to fly in so the greatest danger here is that your drink could finish up in your lap. This comparatively slow flight in weather conditions is what flying was like before the jet.

During the approach phase, which is after aircraft have left the airport entry points, the pilot has to lower his wheels and flaps. We all know what the wheels are about. An aircraft can weigh many tons and it needs an enormously strong undercarriage to support it, especially on touchdown. The hydraulic system which forces this down seems to growl and grumble but we do need it.

The wing flaps are there to increase the wing area so that the aircraft can fly at a lower speed in the later stages and give us a smoother touchdown. So be ready for the whine when they are extended.

And, finally, that noise immediately after touchdown when the engines are put into reverse thrust. This has the same effect as changing down in a car and enables the pilot to slow down with minimum braking. And after that you are home. 'Heathrow Ground this is Speedbird 174 clearing runway 271.' 'Roger Speedbird 174, turn right onto the inner taxiway, your stand C5.'

Chapter 7
ATC at Gatwick Airport

Gatwick is Britain's number two airport; it ranks number two in the world table of international airports and is the busiest single runway airport.

Although Gatwick was designated a public airport as long ago as 1936 it only really began to assume any significance with the building of a concrete runway in 1958. That runway has since been extended to take the big jets, new terminals and stands have been constructed and it has its own railway station with connections to Victoria station in London as well as to various points on BR's Southern Region. It can also be reached by road via the M23 and A23.

Development here has been quite different from that at Heathrow. The terminal buildings are adjacent to the road and rail links, providing direct access for passengers and the whole set-up should be less of a puzzle than Heathrow with its complex of roads and terminal buildings.

The aerodrome layout is comparatively straightforward (Dia 7.1). Many of the stands are adjacent to the terminal building with access via walkways and jetties although some require bussing to and fro. A reasonably uncomplicated system of taxiways connects the stands with the runway which extends for almost two miles into the country. During westerly operations (about seventy per cent of the time) take-offs and landings are on runway 26 which means a short journey to the take-off point but a long one to return to the stand after landing. During easterly operations the position is reversed, of course.

The single runway at Gatwick makes the ATC task rather different from that at Heathrow. All landings and take-offs use the same runway and, whereas Heathrow can space their landing aircraft as little as four miles apart, Gatwick will increase the landing intervals to allow spaces for aircraft to take off. These intervals will vary with the types of aircraft involved; for example, a jumbo entering the runway for take-off will require more time than a light, fast jet and the air controller must co-ordinate with the No 2 director to vary the intervals as required. Getting it all right is quite an art.

Obviously, with only one runway Gatwick can handle less traffic over a period than does Heathrow but there are fewer

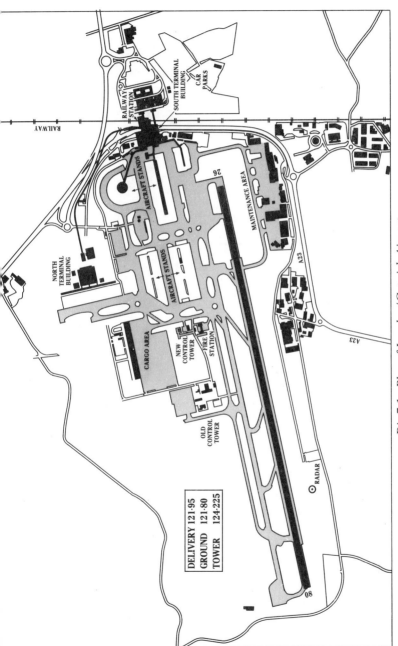

Dia 7.1. Plan of London/Gatwick Airport.

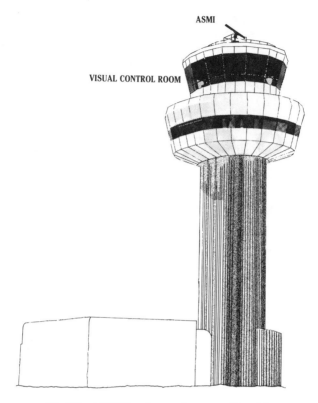

ASMI

VISUAL CONTROL ROOM

Dia 7.2. ATC Visual control room at Gatwick.

controllers involved so the work load is equally high and demanding. The mix of aircraft using the runway and the smaller manoeuvring area bring their own problems and ground planning and movement control can be complicated. Every controller's nightmare is that one day he or she will have two aircraft facing each other at a point where they can't pass and that a tug will have to be called in to resolve the situation. But so far it has not happened.

The Visual Control Room is mounted on a stalk immediately west of the parking area (Dia 7.2). The three controllers involved have a view over the whole of the airport and they have the same radars (DFTI and ASMI) as Heathrow. A lighting operator follows GMC instructions and selects approach, runway and taxi lighting. A teleprinter produces advance warning strips for impending departures and arrivals. Half-hourly weather reports are displayed on CCTV and an anemometer provides a continuous indication of wind speed and direction.

The best teacher in ATC is experience. All ATCOs undergo two years of intensive training at the College of ATC in order to learn the basic ATC rules and procedures on which they are very strictly examined before the issue of CAA licenses to operate at particular types of ATC units. But when they arrive at a unit they have to continue training to 'validate' the license for that unit.

So at Gatwick, as elsewhere, ATCOs start off under training during which time they learn about Gatwick and its methods and procedures from more experienced controllers. Basic standards of separation of aircraft in terms of time, distance or altitude are the same everywhere but each airport is different from any other and it is the differences which are important at this stage. Familiarisation starts in aerodrome control.

All trainee ATCOs will study such things as airport layout, cul-de-sacs and stands, lighting systems and approach aids. They will learn distances, measurements and block numbers and how to operate in every position in the VCR.

When the budding controller knows it all and has proved his competence in every position he will take yet another examination to obtain the validation which will enable him to work alone. This can take several months and the procedure is repeated when, after a period of consolidation in the tower, he moves on to approach control and radar.

Planning the Departures

Gatwick has its own scheduling committee which decides the timetable of arrivals and departures for the various airlines. The operators then file flight plans with ATC but not for individual flights. They can file their whole timetable of flights for the season into the ATC computer which will then extract the details for each departing and arriving flight one hour before the scheduled time and pass them to GMP or Air by teleprinter on cardboard FPSs.

We have looked at the GMP task at Heathrow and there is very little difference at Gatwick except that there is a smaller manoeuvring area and the number started for take-off is even more critical. Aircraft with slot times must, again, be given priority and not blocked in. It would be very embarrassing to get it wrong.

Ground Movement Control

GMC takes over from GMP when the aircraft has started engines and is ready to move. For example, 'Gatwick Ground this is

Caledonian 765, stand 21, push back and taxi clearance'. It is then for GMC to co-ordinate this aircraft with any other aircraft or vehicle on the manoeuvring area, work in progress and all the other things that can happen on an airport. And when the departing aircraft is clear of all the problems and has an unobstructed run to the take-off point the pilot is instructed to contact Air Control on RT.

The Air Controller
It is in the use of the runway itself that Gatwick differs most from Heathrow because it has one runway for both functions and controller technique is quite different: the responsibility here cannot be shared and a single Air Controller handles it all. He (or she) will have some help and will be relieved of much of the routine work, such as telephone liaison with approach control, and his assistant will point out priorities such as departure slots, but he is the star performer and the decisions regarding order and safety rest with him.

What the Air Controller here particularly needs to learn is how to control aircraft of various types and sizes moving at different speeds while landing and taking off on the same runway in good weather or bad, good visibility or fog, by day or by night. Single runway operation demands great concentration, continuous assessment of a constantly changing situation and an ability to make decisions calmly but quickly. The controller watches the runway, either visually or on his ASMI, the holding point and the aircraft approaching it and the DFTI which shows traffic on the approach.

What he aims to do in busy periods is to alternate landings and take-offs, using the runway as efficiently as possible. This requires co-ordination with the No 2 Director so that the spacing between arrivals is right for the type of aircraft which will be departing in particular gaps. Hence the need to watch the aircraft at or approaching the holding point.

As a landing aircraft touches down the controller will clear the next departure to enter the runway and 'hold', having first checked on the DFTI that there is a big enough gap before the next arrival (Dia 7.3). As the landing aircraft clears the runway the departure will be cleared for take-off, by which time the next arrival will be about three miles from touchdown.

When the departure is airborne the next arrival is cleared to land and given a final wind and runway surface check if necessary, and the departure is given his airborne time and instructed to call on the departure frequency (more of this later). By this time the

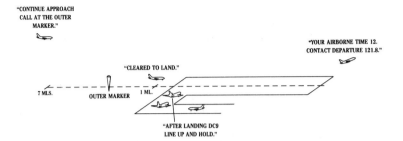

Dia 7.3. Landing/Take-off pattern.

next departure will be waiting for take-off clearance and the next arrival will have called on final approach and will be showing on the DFTI. And so on, sometimes for hours on end.

There may be problems. On a wet runway or in foggy conditions landing aircraft may be slow to clear so the landing intervals must be increased. Large aircraft need more time on the runway than small aircraft. A flight instrument on a departing aircraft may be suspect and the pilot decides not to go. Can that aircraft be cleared off the runway or must the approaching aircraft be instructed to go round again (overshot) and transferred back to approach control for re-sequencing? In fact this almost never happens but the controller must be prepared for any eventuality and always be ready to change his mind and his instructions.

Departure sequencing is much the same as at Heathrow. As aircraft approach the holding point and are transferred from GMC to Air the controller checks the departure route to see whether they will be turning left or right or continuing ahead after take-off and juggles them into the right order. And aircraft which have departure slots may only take off at the allocated time and, so, must have priority.

At Heathrow an aircraft can be cleared onto the runway to hold until a specified time in order to make a departure slot or to achieve the correct time interval behind a preceding aircraft. But not at Gatwick unless there are no landing aircraft. There, departures have to be fitted into the landing stream which makes it difficult to apply time separations between departing aircraft and the intervals are based on a minimum distance of five miles.

When an aircraft is airborne and the take-off time is broadcast, this time is fed into the computer and all the LATCC controllers who will handle the aircraft are immediately presented with the FPSs relevant to that flight. They will then take control as it passes into their sectors.

Approach control and radar

Gatwick ATC is unusual in that aerodrome and approach control are carried out in different buildings. They used to be together in the old control tower shown in Dia 7.1 but a new VCR was commissioned in 1984 and approach control was left in the old building. Controllers alternate between the two so that they remain familiar with all aspects of the ATC operation.

Another slight difference is that Gatwick has two entry points which are not at the locations of VORs. Air traffic here has increased a great deal over the last few years and, whereas it was once enough to have just one entry point via a VOR called Mayfield, a second entry point had to be established to cope with the increased volume. Remember that an entry point is also used for holding aircraft which cannot be fitted into the approach stream and that the stacks extend from 7000ft (seven levels at 1000ft intervals). This was considered not to be enough in case of bad weather delays and a second entry (holding) point was required.

The problem was where to put it. Some re-organization of air routes was possible to release the airspace required for a second holding area but VORs are rather large installations and, not surprisingly, people don't like them in their back gardens or local beauty spots. Fortunately there is a method of holding which does not require a 'dedicated' VOR provided that there is a VOR/DME installation not too far away.

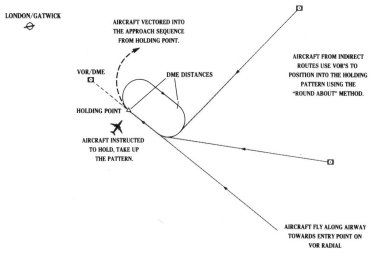

Dia 7.4. VOR/DME entry/holding.

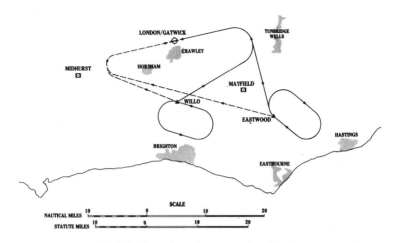

Dia 7.5. Location of Eastwood and Willo.
Approach routes for Easterly _ _ _ _ and Westerly _____ Operations.

We know that a pilot can fly along a VOR radial just as a car
can be driven along a road. If we define a position as a DME
distance from the VOR along the radial we can give that position
a name and designate it as the holding point. Aircraft instructed
to hold will fly to that point and then turn to a reciprocal track to
fly back to a second stated DME distance before turning again to
the inbound radial and the holding point (Dia 7.4). They will
continue to do that, at different altitudes of course, for as long as
instructed.

There are two such entry points for Gatwick named Eastwood
and Willo and they are based on the previously existing VOR/
DMEs at Mayfield and Midhurst. Their locations are shown in
Dia 7.5.

Other than the method of holding, the procedures for aircraft
inbound to Gatwick are just the same as those at Heathrow. They
are cleared by LATCC to the holding points at different altitudes
and control is transferred to Gatwick at those points. Since there
are only two holding points, the north/south sectorization that we
saw at Heathrow is not necessary here and the team consists of
one Approach Controller, one No 1 Director and one No 2
Director.

The Approach Controller remains the link with LATCC
en-route control, he accepts releases on inbound aircraft and
controls the stacks, he double-checks that inbound aircraft will be
at different levels and keeps the FPSs up to date for the benefit of

the No 1 Director and the LATCC TMA controller to whom the display is televised. These strips provide a continuous record of what is happening and any instruction or information passed to the pilot must be noted on them. After use they are retained for a period in case they need to be referred to later.

The No 1 Director makes his own decisions about aircraft cleared to the holding points. He will have a few minutes' advance warning and can watch them as they approach the holding points and plan ahead. He (or she) will issue instructions as to whether an aircraft is to be cleared past the holding point and directed into the approach sequence or instructed to enter the holding pattern. The Approach Controller will clear aircraft in the stack to descend as levels become vacant but after they leave the holding point it is the No 1 who will instruct pilots when to descend and what headings and speeds to fly until the initial sequence is set up, when he will transfer control to the No 2 Director.

We already know about No 2 Directors. They provide the precision required to ensure the most efficient use of the runway and, at single runway airports particularly, they must liaise with the Air controllers who will specify the spacing required. Since the spacing depends on the type of departing aircraft as much as on the aircraft ahead (as at Heathrow) this makes the No 2's job quite difficult.

When the No 2 is happy with the spacing and the aircraft is flying at the right speed to maintain it, the pilot is told to contact the Air controller who will then accept responsibility for the safety of the aircraft and we are back into the aerodrome control cycle.

There is another radar controller in approach who has not been mentioned yet, the No 3 Director who is, in fact, a departure controller. Some Gatwick departures will be transferred to LATCC as soon as they are airborne. However, there are routes which turn back towards the final approach side of the airport and aircraft using those routes are retained by Gatwick approach. When they are airborne, and before turning back to fly north of the airport, they are transferred to the No 3 who will in turn release them to LATCC when there is no further interaction with inbound traffic.

Chapter 8
Luton International Airport

Luton International Airport is an important part of London's airport complex. It has, for many years, specialized in charter holiday flights and has two major airlines based there which are heavily involved in that type of business. A number of other charter operators, both British and foreign, utilise the facilities.

More recently, scheduled flights have become an increasingly important part of Luton's operations. Since a relaxation of fare controls and granting of route licences, one independent Irish airline has developed Luton as the United Kingdom destination for its many services from and to Ireland. Other airlines have followed this lead with services developing between Europe and Luton, and between airports within the United Kingdom.

Luton also accommodates a leading business aviation charter company, freight operations, taxi services, mail services and a flying club. So, although Luton Airport is truly international in the sense that it is a holiday and business gateway for millions of passengers, it is also very much a regional airport offering services to local commerce and business interests. Their Air Traffic Control Unit is the largest independent unit in Europe. The ATC and telecommunications staff are employed directly by the Airport Company, but they are all qualified and licensed in the same way as the CAA staff and their standards are second to none.

The Airport is a limited company, wholly owned by Luton Borough Council. The equipment and facilities are of a very high order and the operators are determined that Luton will remain in the forefront of modern airports. Passengers will be interested to know that Luton has a new terminal building which provides a very efficient level of service for passenger handling and has the scope for the increases envisaged for the rest of the century; there are already plans for extensions. There are plentiful bus, coach and train services and large car parking areas and the whole atmosphere of the airport is friendly and relaxing. Even spectators are well catered for in a separate, specially designed building which has a buffet and bar.

Luton has one runway which is over 7000 feet long and 150 feet wide (Dia 8.1). There is a single taxiway to and from the parking

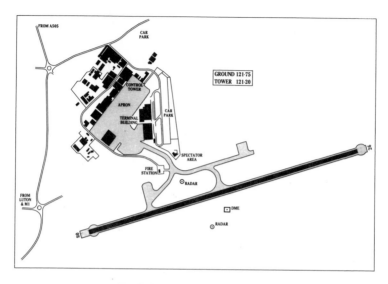

Dia 8.1. Luton Airport Layout.

apron which splits into two to join the runway at the centre rather than at each end, as at most airports, and the controllers have to be very precise about how they clear aircraft in and out between the stands and the runway. This layout also means that aircraft taking off will usually have to enter the runway and back-track to the take-off point and that aircraft landing will often have to turn 180° on the runway and back-track to the exit. When this is happening the gaps between landing aircraft must be greater than at Gatwick, for example; this means a lower runway movement rate but with greater complexity, calling for constant liaison between all the controllers concerned. However, they are very well organized and the pilots, too, know the problems and co-operate fully to ensure a smooth operation. But there will be changes here, too; the Airport Company has plans for developing the layout to include a parallel taxiway and new aprons and parking stands.

As at other airports, ATC is divided into two sections, aerodrome control in the visual control room and approach control on a lower floor (Dia 8.2). The tower is due for replacement but a measure of the standard of equipment is that Luton was only the second airport in the UK (after Heathrow) to be equipped with Secondary Radar (SSR) to complement their excellent primary radar. ATC service is provided for 24 hours per day by up to five ATCOs at a time on a shift-working basis.

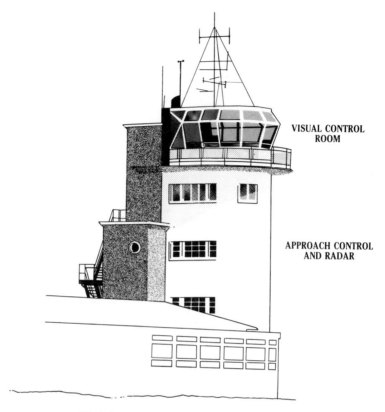

VISUAL CONTROL
ROOM

APPROACH CONTROL
AND RADAR

Dia 8.2. The control tower at Luton Airport.

The tower does not control just the airport. Luton has its own Control Zone/Special Rules Zone to ensure protection down to ground level for aircraft landing and taking off, and its own Control Area/Special Rules Area to protect aircraft in the transition phase between Luton Zone and the LTMA (Airport Zones and Areas are sometimes dual-designated for legal reasons which need not concern the reader). Diagram 8.3 shows this airspace and its relationship to the LTMA and Stansted airspace.

No aircraft may enter this airspace except on a co-ordinated transfer from another ATC authority, eg, LTMA or Stansted, or with the direct permission of Luton approach control. So Luton controls the airport and the surrounding airspace; the inbound/outbound routes for airline traffic connect directly with LTMA airspace, while aircraft flying outside the airways system, such as taxi or private aircraft, will call Luton Approach for permission to

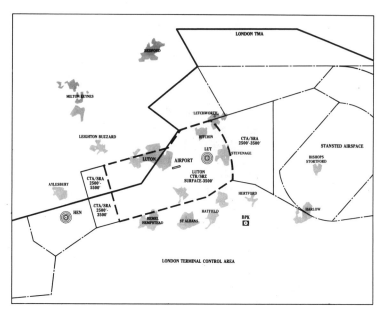

Dia 8.3. Luton's Airspace – and its relationship to the LTMA and Stansted.

enter. Luton also provides a service to aircraft which may wish to cross the SRA or SRZ in transit between other airports and even to traffic flying close to their airspace and requesting a general surveillance or advisory service. Obviously all air traffic in the area is of interest to Luton controllers and they are happy to enhance the local safety level by providing such a service.

Now we can look at the arrival routes for Luton airport and here we have a slight problem. The LTMA in the Luton and Stansted areas is currently being re-organized and there may well be further changes in the not too distant future. It seems better to disregard the changes and to explain the system as it was before October 1988; at least the principles are much the same.

There is a VOR called Barkway within Stansted's airspace (Dia 8.4) and the inbound routes for both Luton and Stansted were aligned on that beacon. If aircraft were required to hold for either airport they would do so at Barkway where they would be controlled by Stansted Approach. When a Luton inbound was able to commence its approach from the holding pattern it would be vectored out of the pattern by Stansted and handed over to Luton as it entered Luton airspace, clear of all Stansted traffic.

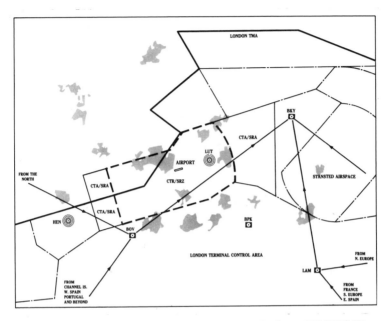

Dia 8.4. Standard inbound routes to Luton via Barkway VOR/DME.

In fact, very few Luton inbounds have ever got as far as Barkway. Luton radar can see aircraft well outside its own airspace and can identify the traffic using SSR. There is a very close liaison between LTMA controllers and Luton approach radar controllers and most aircraft were positioned by TMA for direct 'radar handovers' to Luton so that Barkway could be bypassed and the aircraft vectored straight into the Luton approach sequence.

The reason that all this is being changed is that both airports are being developed, traffic will increase and it will be necessary for the airports to have separate holding patterns, or at least a different arrangement from that which they have had in the past.

Outbound routes into the airways system are, as at other airports, published as Standard Instrument Departure Routes (SIDs) so that everyone concerned will know precisely the routes to be followed and the altitudes to be achieved by specified positions (Dia 8.5). Luton radar is responsible for separating departures from arriving aircraft and when those departures are clear of all other Luton traffic they are transferred to LATCC's TMA(N) for entry into the airways system in co-ordination with

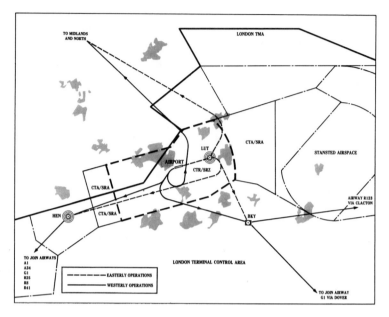

Dia 8.5. Luton's departure routes.

all other aircraft under LATCC control.

We have looked at Luton in rather less detail than Heathrow and Gatwick to avoid repetition of the basics of ATC but the greatest difference between the three is one of size. Luton is the smallest but its reputation is as good as any and it is known in the trade as a great little airport (but getting bigger).

Chapter 9
Stansted Airport

Stansted Airport or, to give it its full title, London/Stansted Airport, has had a varied career. Built by the American Air Force in 1942 it was used by them for the remainder of the war mainly as a maintenance base, although it housed a light bomber wing for a period in 1944. After the war it was handed to the RAF who used it for storage and disposal of wartime equipment; it was taken over by the Ministry of Civil Aviation in 1949 and passed to the British Airports Authority on its formation in 1966.

Stansted has always been rather different from the other airports and it has never really taken off as a major provider of scheduled or charter operations. A number of civil airline operators have come and gone. The names of some have passed into aviation history while others have moved on for reasons of economy or change in demand. A few remain and there is a limited number of scheduled services, mainly using the smaller airlines, while some airlines operate charter flights to such places as Scandinavia, North America, Spain and the Canaries. There is a growing number of freight, executive and taxi flights as well as a fair amount of private flying.

Until the early 1980s some airlines used Stansted for crew training and most types of civil transport aircraft could be seen there but the excellence and realism of modern flight simulators has limited the amount of live training and the big jets are seen less often.

Through it all the airport has always been the home of the Civil Aviation Authority Flying Unit (albeit under various names). This is the unit which is responsible for the flight checking of such things as civil VORs, NDBs, ILSs and radars and it does so not only in the UK but also under contract to some foreign governments. Its pilots also examine other pilots for various qualifications which are required for the more advanced categories of pilot licensing and they are also involved in the testing, assessment and acceptance of new navigation and landing aids.

Stansted has a single runway over 9000ft long (Dia 9.1) and is equipped with radar for approach control and with ILS for landings on runway 23. Landing aircraft on runway 05 which require assistance to line up on the approach are radar vectored

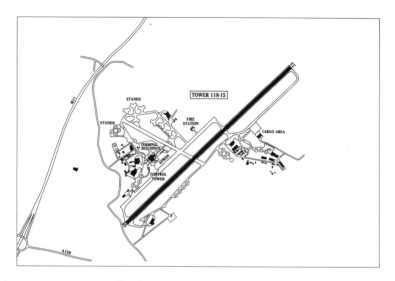

Dia 9.1. Stansted Airport layout.

until they can see the approach lights and/or the runway. The arrangement of the parking stands is rather less than ideal but this

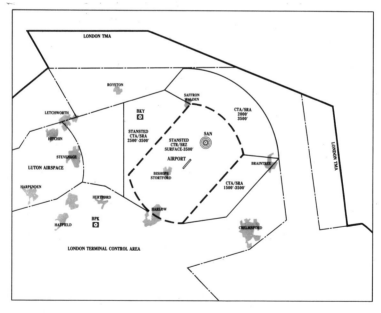

Dia 9.2. Stansted controlled and special rules airspace.

is a legacy of the war when aircraft parking areas were known as dispersals and were just that.

The control tower has the normal layout with aerodrome control in the glass box on the top, with approach and radar control on the floor below.

As at Luton, Stansted has its own Control Zone/Special Rules Zone and Control Area/Special Rules Area (Dia 9.2) which are controlled by Stansted ATCOs and are out of bounds to any aircraft which have not been given permission to enter. The airspace is designed to fit onto and into the north-eastern corner of the LTMA and Airway R123 which serves the outbound route from the LTMA to Holland, Scandinavia, Northern Europe and beyond.

The inbound routes for Stansted have also been changed slightly but, as with Luton, we can look at the way it was and Dia 8.4 shows that, historically, the routes terminated at Barkway VOR. Again, few arriving aircraft ever got to Barkway and were handed over from LTMA radar to Stansted radar for shorter routings and more direct approaches. The formal procedure has changed a little and will change again but radar to radar transfers will continue to be a feature when the traffic situation permits.

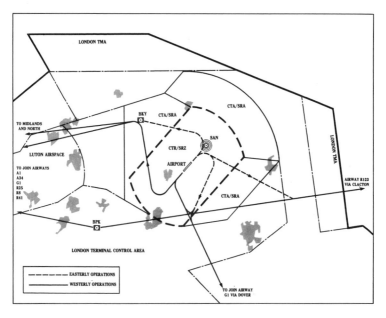

Dia 9.3. Stansted's departure routes.

Outbound routes from Stansted are shown in Dia 9.3. They are published as SIDs and, although they may appear to conflict with outbound routes from other airports, altitude separation is used again when necessary. It is then for the LTMA controllers to decide when aircraft should be cleared to climb above the SID altitudes to enter the en route sectors for further climb to cruising levels. This may be quite soon after take-off in the case of aircraft going to the north or via Airway R123 but those flying around the London area to the north or east may be held down to about 5000ft for quite long distances until they are clear of inbound routes or the Bovingdon and Lambourne holding areas.

So much for the past and the present: the future for Stansted looks very different indeed. The Government has decided that the airport is to be developed in stages and this will mean a complete modernization of buildings and facilities and improvements in such things as navigation and landing aids. The existing runway will remain but, probably, not much else. Road and rail access will be improved. To what extent Stansted will be developed remains to be seen. There is more to it than building a bigger airport, and the constraints could be in the ability of the ATC system to cope with a major increase in air traffic movements generated from an airport in that position. We shall have to wait and see.

Chapter 10
London City Airport

London City Airport is something else. Promoted, developed, built, owned and operated by contractors and civil engineers John Mowlem and Company, it is sited on the central quay between the old Royal Albert and George V docks (Dia 10.1) with the approval of the London Docklands Development Corporation.

The vision behind the project was the provision of frequent air services between the City and the surrounding area and other centres of finance and industry within a radius of about 400 miles from London, an area with a population of about 150 million. The whole of the UK lies within this range and Dia 10.2 shows London's geographic relationship to some of the major European cities. Clearly, there is also some scope here for tourism.

The problems were siting, airport size and, that old bogey, noise. There would not have been a lot of point in building a new airport farther from the City than Heathrow and there had to be enough space for a runway usable by commercially viable aircraft with the necessary terminal buildings, car parks, etc. Since space was bound to be limited there had also to be a reasonably sized

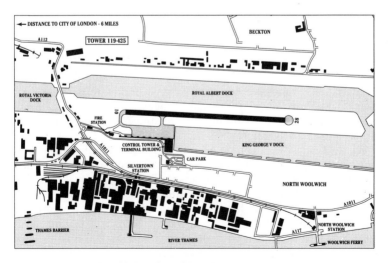

Dia 10.1. Plan of London/City Airport.

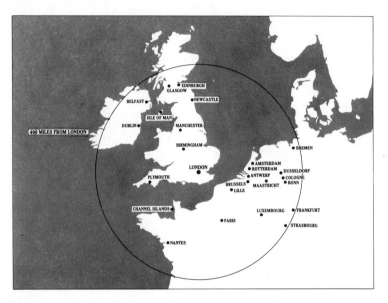

Dia 10.2. The area of operations.

aircraft which could operate off a short runway and make fairly steep approaches and climb-outs. And those aircraft had to be quiet.

The docks area was closed to maritime traffic in 1981 and the Mowlem promotion began then. The site that was considered most suitable was only six miles (a taxi ride) from the City as against Heathrow's sixteen miles (Dia 10.1). Mowlem were supported by Brymon Airways which had years of experience operating an aircraft which was particularly suitable for use in a restricted environment, the DHC Dash 7, and is, moreover, very quiet. The Dash 7 was specifically designed with a STOL (Short Take-Off and Landing) capability and the City airport is often referred to as a STOLport.

We will not dwell too much on the terminal building. It is enough to say that the interior is said to resemble a hotel rather than an airport terminal and that the compact scale of the operation reduces check-in and boarding times, not to mention the quicker get-away after landing. Being an international airport, passengers will be pleased to know that there will be the usual duty-free and tax-free goods on sale for those going to foreign parts. It is probably of interest, too, that in addition to the airport requirements there is also a business centre having conference rooms with modern communications and data centres and that the catering facilities both here and in the terminal are very up-market.

But on to the Air Traffic Control aspect and this is quite interesting. The runway lies in an east/west direction and is about half a mile long. Not much compared to the conventional airports but quite adequate for the types of aircraft that will use this airport. There is a small control tower on the top of the terminal building manned by CAA controllers who have an excellent view of the airport and its approaches, but approach control is carried out from a pair of radar consoles in Heathrow approach control. This ensures that there is perfect co-ordination between controllers and will allow City aircraft to transit Heathrow airspace under positive control when the traffic situation permits but, in any case, to be positioned and sequenced into City's small control zone which extends from the surface to the base of the LTMA.

Much of the airport ATC equipment has been designed specifically for a STOLport. Whereas the ILS glidepath for a standard airport has an approach angle of 3°, London City has a glidepath of 7½° so that aircraft can carry out safe approaches well clear of tall buildings and other obstructions. Pilots have Racal Avionics to thank for that.

The lighting systems for the runways, taxi areas and apron were designed by GEC Electrical Projects and they required particular expertise because the airport must be easily identifiable in such a high density area but the lights must not dazzle pilots. There is also special equipment to measure weather conditions and transmit them automatically to pilots and ATC, courtesy of Marconi Command and Control Systems.

The airport became operational in October 1987 with seven aircraft stands but with room for ten and when all ten are in use the capacity will be 1.2 million passengers per year. So, you see, this is a well considered, very much up-to-date and highly efficient project. Its very uniqueness has demanded some original thinking and the result could well prove to be a 'businessman's delight' for the City of London. That is certainly the declared aim of both Mowlem and the user airlines.

STOP PRESS. During the summer of 1988 landing trials were carried out using the BA146 ultra quiet jet aircraft. If, as is possible, this aircraft is cleared to use London City, a runway extension will be required.

Chapter 11
Flow Control

Flow control is an emotive subject, particularly for those who have had to wait in overcrowded airport terminals for hours, or even days in some cases. Almost everyone in the air transport industry has been blamed for the problems; the CAA, tour operators, airlines, airports at home and abroad, governments, ATCOs you name it. There is general agreement on two points. It is largely a holiday season problem and it is getting worse.

This seasonal effect is a problem which is not confined to the air transport industry. We are all familiar with congested roads during holiday periods, particularly when masses of cars are converging on something like a racecourse, or even a resort. Our road system has improved greatly over the years but even when en route traffic can flow quite well we still see destination bottlenecks. When a number of major roads flow into a single entry road, we have the same problem. Roads have capacities and when these are exceeded, at best we have to slow to a crawl and at worst we have to stop.

It is the same for air travellers. When too many aircraft wish to go to a particular airport or area the local capacities could be exceeded. If countries A, B and C are trying to feed aircraft from their airways systems into the airways of country D, then almost inevitably in peak periods the result will be unacceptable congestion for country D. After all, there is only so much airspace over each country.

Cars and coaches can crawl or stop but this is not an option which is available to aircraft. A pilot can slow down a little, but not enough to make a significant difference. The air equivalent of stopping is to hold, but to allow aircraft to get airborne and then instruct them to hold en route could lead to all sorts of problems. A holding aircraft is blocking a level for other aircraft which may wish to go through so if you have a few aircraft holding the whole system is fouled up. Aircraft held en route could run short of fuel and have to divert to take on more, and then have to try to get back into the stream.

This would become very untidy and ATCOs do not like untidy situations; in fact, they dislike them so much that they will not allow them to happen where they can be foreseen. Controllers are more likely to become overloaded if such things are permitted and both they and their supervisors have a duty to keep things under control. That is what it is all about.

So for any destination airport or area, or for any 'choke-point' en route, the relevant ATCC may impose flow control to regulate the traffic to a safe rate. They do not set out to be unduly restrictive so that their controllers can sit around with their feet up; they simply wish to ensure that no more aircraft flow into the airspace than can be handled safely. They are responding to possible congestion in the only way they can and other ATC authorities must restrict their departures to conform to a given flow rate.

From the ATC point of view, that is it. The question is 'why does it happen?' and this is exercising a lot of minds at the moment. Are there enough airways? Are there enough qualified ATCOs? Is ATC too fragmented and nationalistic and should there be one authority and one employer for the whole of Europe?

What about airports? Are there enough of them in the right places? Do existing airports have all the equipment and staff that they should have? Do they have enough parking space? If an airport can park only ten aircraft and it takes an hour to turn an arrival round for departure, then the highest possible landing rate can be no more than ten per hour, and if fifteen aircraft are scheduled for four consecutive hours you finish up with a two hour delay. Lack of staff such as customs officers can also have a delaying effect.

And airlines and tour operators? Do they know the capacities of the airspace and airports into which they wish to operate? Are they saturating one area one day and another on a different day? Is it possible to have different change-over days at all resorts? Would it be better to have some aircraft based at the resorts so that a bi-directional operation could start each morning?

And governments? Are they planning far enough ahead? Are they allowing more and more hotels to be built before the air transport infrastructure is available? Are they training sufficient staff?

It is stressed very strongly indeed that these are not accusations. They are simply questions that have been asked, very largely by the media.

Who might be blamed? Perhaps no-one specifically. The real villain of the piece seems to be the lack of any Europe-wide organization which could tackle the problem as a whole. An airport scheduling committee is provided with figures which must not be exceeded and they are able to meet and plan their timetables. It has been suggested that European government tourist authorities, tour operators, airlines, ATC and others in the air transport industry should also meet with an urgent brief to discover the problems, decide on some figures and provide the answers. It will take time.

And the cost? It could mean higher fares. If new equipment and facilities, more or improved airports, bigger aircraft, etc, are deemed necessary, the travelling public might have to pay a little more.

As far as the airlines are concerned, flow control can seriously affect the health of both the companies and their employees. It causes many, many problems. The timing of flights was probably organized months earlier and crews usually rostered for flights up to a month ahead. Aircraft and crews will usually make more than one flight per day and if the first of them is delayed then there are two immediate worries. Will the aircraft be able to carry out the day's quota before the night curfew imposed by some airports and will the crew be able to carry out the return journey, or the second flight, within the permitted duty time? (Crew's duty hours are strictly limited for safety reasons.) A further worry is that no-one yet knows what the delays are likely to be at the other end and the situation might get worse.

And there could be a knock-on effect. An aircraft might be scheduled for a first trip to an area where there are restrictions and to a second where there are none; if it returns late from trip one, the passengers for area two will also suffer a delay. And don't say that there should be spare aircraft standing by just in case unless you are prepared to pay (in your fare) for extra aircraft which cost millions of pounds but don't earn their keep. It's not feasible.

A common complaint from passengers is that the airlines do not keep them advised of the situation, that there is no 'communication'. But how can the airline communicate when it does not, itself, know what is going on? If an aircraft started its day with a delay in the UK and is now subject to an indefinite delay at an airport hundreds of miles away, it would appear that no-one knows or could know. The crew is running out of duty time and the airline may have to find another crew to take the aircraft out when it does return. Is there another crew available and has it had the required break since its last duty period? What time should they be called in? There are always some standby crews in case of sickness, etc, but the companies can hardly cater for the unknown. It is a worrying and stressful time for all concerned.

Not the least so for that poor girl on the desk who has to try to cope with the full force of delayed passenger fury when she probably knows no more than they do. There is no point in getting angry and shouting at her. Please do not take it out on the counter staff: they have their own problems and you would not want to bring forward their nervous breakdowns!

Meanwhile, there are flow control units at most of the European ATCCs. In the UK the Departure Flow Regulator (DFR) is at LATCC and is, in fact, a specialized team of ATCOs. At the beginning of the day all the ATCCs will telex details of any restrictions which may be in force for the day; the ATCCs will then advise all airports and airline operators in their areas and instruct them to request departure slots for any aircraft wishing to take off for any of the specified routes or destination airports.

In addition, DFR may impose some departure restrictions of his own so as to allow him to plan an even flow of traffic along an airway with no 'bunching'. In such cases the delays may be only slight, pilots might call for start clearance from the aircraft and GMP will contact DFR and obtain a departure slot time. So the aircraft could have to wait on the stand for a few minutes but that is no real problem.

Where foreign delays are likely to be significant the airlines themselves may 'phone DFR up to four hours ahead of the planned departure time to ascertain the situation and ask for a departure slot. If this means that there will be a considerable delay, an airline then has time to contact the crew and instruct it not to report for duty until the time it will be required. The crew duty day then starts from the later time.

A complication for DFR is that other ATCCs may define restrictions in two forms. One may specify that aircraft on a particular airway will be accepted at, perhaps, two different levels but not less than fifteen minutes apart at each level (standard separation at ATCC boundaries is ten minutes). They may go on to say that aircraft going beyond a certain point must be not less than thirty minutes apart (because of further restrictions along the airway) and/or that aircraft landing at airport A in their area must be not less than ten minutes apart and at airport B not less than twenty minutes apart (to avoid airport congestion) while there is no restriction on aircraft landing at airport C (but the en route restrictions still apply). There may be different restrictions for other routes, but given in the same form.

Other ATCCs may require a telephone request for each individual aircraft entering their airspace and they may then have to 'phone the next en route ATCC to agree onward clearance for that aircraft before 'phoning it back to the originator.

With practice the first type of restriction is not too difficult for DFR provided he has a brain like a computer. He works out his boundary slots, refers to an FPS for the en route time from take-off to the boundary and calculates that back to give a departure slot. The aircraft must then be airborne within six minutes of that time or the slot is lost. The (mental) computation is the same whether the aircraft is from Glasgow or Gatwick and aircraft must fit into the boundary slots. Mistakes are not acceptable and remember that DFR may be regulating a number of airways and working some hours ahead.

The second type of restriction is harder on DFR's nerves. He knows what time the aircraft can depart the airport and how long it will take to the boundary. He has the usual stack of FPSs and can see if and when boundary slots may be available. He then passes his request to the next ATCC, hoping for an immediate reply and clearance. But he might have to wait some time while the clock ticks on, sometimes even to the point when the aircraft can no longer make the time requested. Frustration, re-calculation, another 'phone call.

Meanwhile the airline is getting desperate and pleading for a slot over which DFR has no control. It is a nasty situation and DFR knows that he is on a good hiding to nothing. He sometimes feels that he is the least understood and most unloved ATCO in the trade and longs for going home time. This is true (if tongue in cheek, perhaps).

Passengers aren't the only people who feel strongly about delays. The airlines do. Their employees do. ATCOs do — and certainly DFRs do. The latter work very hard to ensure maximum efficiency within the situation that is presented to them and they feel particularly strongly about lost slots.

The lost slot seems to be something which is not fully understood but DFR is trained to retrieve it where possible. He cannot always so do but his hatred of the lost slot gives him a special incentive to try.

If the slot is lost at an airport where the aircraft for the next slot has arrived early at the same runway, a quick switch where 2 becomes 1 and vice versa may retrieve the situation and reinstate the slot. However, if there is no second aircraft waiting at the same airport and runway there is a problem — but it might yet be resolved. Not if it happens at Gatwick, but if the slot is lost at Birmingham or any point north of that then it is possible that an aircraft from an airport further south might be brought forward to fill it. The slot originally allocated to the filler-in may then be given to the slot-loser and, so, nothing is lost after all. This gives

DFR a warm glow because he is a very helpful fellow really but it is hard work requiring some rapid calculations and a bit of luck.

The serious point is that if an aircraft misses its slot it may sometimes be possible to do a bit of switching to retrieve the situation but, perhaps more often than not, the slot is lost. Aircraft allocated the following slots may be from airports more distant from the boundary and could be already airborne. There will also be other aircraft loading or taxiing, crews coming in at their new times, delayed passengers being called. The only stage at which the aircraft with the lost slot can be fitted in again is at the end of the queue, and that could be hours away.

Passengers should be particularly careful that they answer calls for boarding when requested so that they do not cause slots to be missed. Those responsible for requesting slots should be aware of the implications because a lost slot resulting in a further delay is a tragedy for passengers, crews and airlines.

There have been some unfortunate public statements regarding flow control. One is that northern airports are at a disadvantage compared with those in the London area, the implication appearing to be that London's airports are given preferential treatment. This is quite untrue. Slots are allocated strictly in the order in which they are requested, regardless of the airport. It is thought that such statements might encourage those requesting departure times from northern airports to jump the gun in the belief that they will be pushed back in the queue anyway, and this can lead to slots being lost because optimistically early times have been asked for.

A second, rather mysterious, pronouncement first heard in 1988 was that while some airports were suffering delays, others had spare slots available. Very odd. Slots are not allocated to or by airports: they are given by LATCC only to particular aircraft, no matter at which airport they may be.

However, these statements could be due to a misunderstanding of the situation and might not mean quite what they seem to. By agreement between ATCCs, Route Orientation Schemes may come into effect during the summer period and this means that traffic from a particular area, such as London, will use one pre-arranged route, while those from another area will use another route, and all in the interest of simplification. We can look at the scheme from the UK to the Iberian Peninsular and the Canaries and we see that aircraft from Manchester and airports to the north of it avoid the London area by flying south from Manchester and crossing Cardiff and Brixham *en route* to the Channel Isles and beyond. Aircraft from Birmingham, East Midlands and airports to the south of them bound for Spain leave the UK at points between Bognor Regis and Seaford, and fly almost due south to join an entirely different route through French airspace. Aircraft from those more southerly airports for Portugal and the Canaries leave the UK in the Southampton area to merge with aircraft from Northern and Scottish airports over Brittany and the Channel Isles. France has similar agreements with the countries of northern Europe which also wish to send aircraft to Spain and beyond. That might give some idea of the complexity of the situation.

Misunderstandings may arise because each route is regulated separately and there will sometimes be an imbalance between the routes. Aircraft from northern airports may sometimes suffer longer delays than those from southern airports, but it could well be the other way round. Unfortunately the route orientation system is rather inflexible and aircraft cannot normally be switched from one route to another during periods of imbalance, but ATC is working on it. Meanwhile we can't make direct comparisons.

It is difficult to follow the reasoning of those who claim that the answer to holiday delays is the provision of more runways and terminal facilities, particularly in the south-east. If the foreign destination airports and ATC systems are unable to accept the number of aircraft generated by the UK and others at present, it would seem that the launching of more aircraft into already congested areas would have quite horrifying results for passengers unless the whole system is better managed so that the hourly delivery rate matches the hourly acceptance rate.

Long delays are a bit of a nightmare all round, but the biggest nightmare for everyone involved is industrial action which is invariably taken at the busiest periods for maximum effect. You can only pray that this doesn't hit you.

One thing that passengers find particularly annoying is that they are expected to check in on time even when there are known delays. There is a good reason for this: check-in desks are reserved for flights as scheduled and to attempt to change the programme at the last moment could lead to an awful mix-up of baggage and passengers. In any case, how could passengers be contacted and given revised check-in times? There seems no way out of this, so don't 'phone in to check. Just arrive on time and hope.

Chapter 12
The London Air Traffic
Control Centre

The concept of air traffic control at an airport is reasonably straightforward but an Air Traffic Control Centre is an entirely different ball-game. At an airport one can see aircraft landing, taking off and taxiing but at a Centre they are represented only by the inevitable flight progress strips and blips on radar screens. A controller posted to a Centre after having served at an airport might well miss all the activity and could find it rather abstract but the purpose remains the same (to quote from the ATC bible, 'the safe and expeditious conduct of flights') and he, or she, will soon accept the differences and settle down.

And there are differences. The airport controller works in a comparatively restricted airspace with aircraft which are seldom flying at more than 250 knots. The Centre controller, particularly the en route controller, operates over much greater distances with aircraft which either could be cruising at speeds of up to 500 knots but, unless over-flying, will reduce speed progressively to 250 knots as they approach the airport entry points or, if outbound, will be climbing at the lower speeds but increasing to cruising speeds at the top of the climb. Again, aircraft at the lower (airport) levels can be controlled to some extent by instructing pilots to fly at standard speeds but such speed control is seldom used at the higher levels and a different technique is required.

The two aspects of the job are known as either aerodrome and approach control or area control and, although the tasks are quite different, the application and concentration required are much the same.

The London Air Traffic Control Centre (LATCC) is by far the largest unit in the UK. It has about five times as many controllers as Heathrow, including a very much bigger support staff. In addition some of the services provided by LATCC telecommunications engineers and computer staffs are piped through to airport units.

LATCC controls not only the airspace known as the London Terminal Control Area (LTMA) which encompasses the control zones around the various London airports, but also the whole of the airways system south of the Scottish border which connects UK airports to the airways systems of the other countries around us (See Dia 2.1). It accepts departures from UK airports and sees them on their way to foreign as well as domestic destinations and it accepts arrivals from adjacent ATCCs which are either inbound to airports in its area or will overfly through the LATCC airways system, eg, between Scotland and Europe or North America and Europe.

The controllers work in quite different surroundings from those at airports. LATCC consists of a very large operations room (Dia 12.1) with a watch manager's desk at one end and a line of control suites plus teleprinters for the various sectors along each side. Because of the complexity and sheer volume of the *en route* structure, controllers can hardly be expected to know it all in detail and so the airspace is sectorized (Dia 12.2) and one controller may work in up to four sectors. The control suites conform to those sectors and different suites have different radar displays. Military controllers have a control suite in this ops room (not shown) and

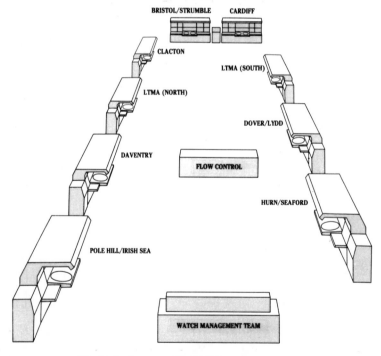

Dia 12.1. Layout of LATCC operations room.

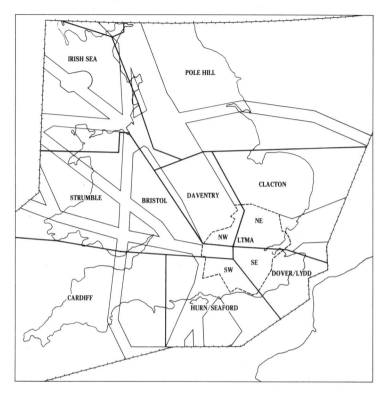

Dia 12.2. London ATCC airspace sectorization.

they also work on various civil suites to co-ordinate airways crossings by military aircraft.

Flow regulation is also carried out here. In Chapter 11 we considered the system and some of the problems which made it necessary. It used to be a one-man operation but more and more ATCOs have had to be allocated to this particular task and it is a real headache of a job. We know that DFR has a responsibility to airports, airlines and passengers but he is also aware of his responsibility to sector controllers who depend on him for the correct flow rate at the boundaries. DFR is very much a part of the LATCC system which we can talk about now.

The TMA Sectors
We have looked at the individual airports in the London area and now we can begin at LATCC by looking at those sectors which

accept aircraft from, or transfer aircraft to, the airports, and these are the TMA (Terminal Control Area) sectors.

For control purposes the TMA is divided into north and south sectors (remember Heathrow) and they work on different control suites (Dia 12.1). Each suite is further divided into two sectors, east and west, and each of these sectors has two controllers, one to control inbound and one to control outbound traffic. In addition each control suite will have a fifth controller known as the Crew Chief who does not contact aircraft but acts as a co-ordinator between the TMA sectors and the airports and en route sectors. He also deals with such things as equipment or other problems which might distract radar controllers.

LTMA airspace can be likened to an irregular-shaped box surrounding the airport zones and extending upwards from a general base of 2500ft (although some of the outer sections are higher) to an upper limit of 13,000ft. The route system within the

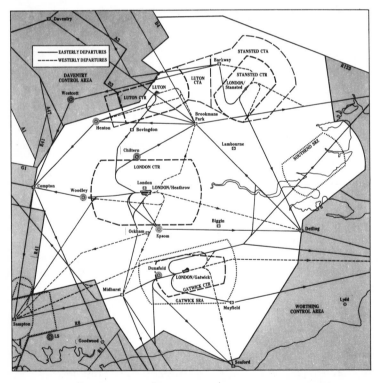

Dia 12.3. Standard departure routes in the London TMA.

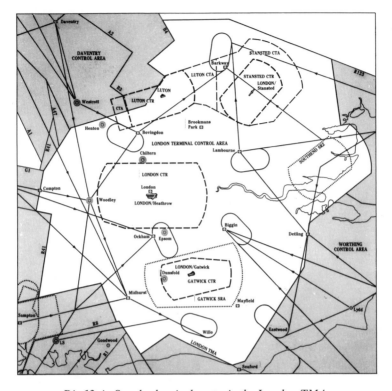

Dia 12.4. Standard arrival routes in the London TMA.

TMA is necessarily complex because all of London's airports handle traffic from and to all directions. Just how complex can be seen in Diagrams 12.3 and 12.4 which show separately the inbound and outbound routes, but remember that the airspace is quartered and that each quarter is controlled by two ATCOs so that the problems are shared.

The difficulty is that, because of the multi-directional operations, some inbound and outbound routes must cross and some will merge but we do have the third dimension of altitude and this is applied so that where routes do cross or merge they will do so quite safely at different altitudes. Dia 12.5 shows this for the LTMA (SW) sector.

The general principle is that aircraft inbound to the airport entry points will be cleared to descend in the *en route* sectors to the top of the TMA airspace (13,000ft) and control will then be transferred to the appropriate inbound TMA controller (Dia

12.6). He will have seen the aircraft approaching on his radar but will know from the approach control closed circuit television (CCTV) display how many aircraft, if any, are in the entry point holding patterns and what levels they are occupying so he can continue to clear the aircraft down to the available levels while vectoring them to remain at least five miles clear of each other until vertical separation has been achieved. He will have told

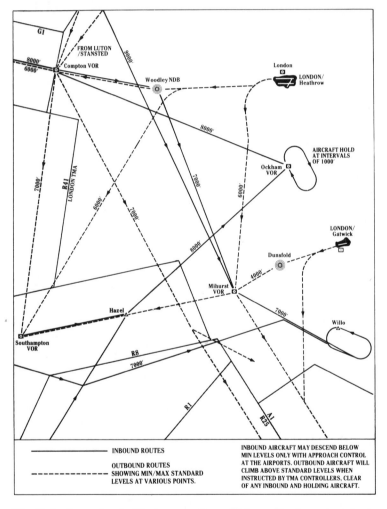

Dia 12.5. Example of altitude separation of inbound/outbound routes in the LTMA (SW) sector.

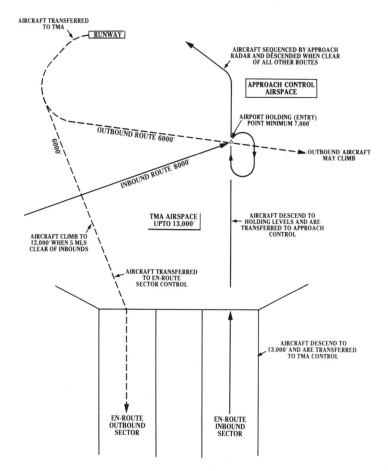

AIRCRAFT TRANSFERRED
TO TMA

RUNWAY

AIRCRAFT SEQUENCED BY APPROACH
RADAR AND DESCENDED WHEN CLEAR
OF ALL OTHER ROUTES

APPROACH CONTROL
AIRSPACE

AIRPORT HOLDING (ENTRY)
POINT MINIMUM 7,000'

OUTBOUND ROUTE 6000'

6000

OUTBOUND AIRCRAFT
MAY CLIMB

INBOUND ROUTE 8000'

TMA AIRSPACE
UPTO 13,000'

AIRCRAFT DESCEND TO
HOLDING LEVELS AND ARE
TRANSFERRED TO APPROACH
CONTROL

AIRCRAFT CLIMB TO
12,000' WHEN 5 MLS
CLEAR OF INBOUNDS

AIRCRAFT TRANSFERRED
TO EN-ROUTE
SECTOR CONTROL

AIRCRAFT DESCEND TO
13,000' AND ARE TRANSFERRED
TO TMA CONTROL

EN-ROUTE
OUTBOUND
SECTOR

EN-ROUTE
INBOUND
SECTOR

Dia 12.6. The outbound/inbound procedures between TMA and en route sectors.

approach control of the order of arrival and the allocated levels and when aircraft have achieved those levels he can clear them to continue direct to the entry point and transfer them to approach control. We already know that approach control and radar at the airport will control the stack and how they do that and direct aircraft into the approach sequence.

Aircraft outbound from the airports will be transferred to a TMA outbound controller as soon as possible after take-off when they are clear of all other airport traffic (Dia 12.6). We have also seen that there is a time or distance interval between departures and that this may vary depending on aircraft speed (two minutes or five miles at the same speed, increased if the following aircraft is faster) and this ensures a safe distance apart on transfer.

Aircraft follow standard departure routes (more of this later) and the altitudes at various points along the route are also specified. Since these altitudes build in separation at points where routes will merge or cross and will always be below the altitudes specified for inbound routes, it might be thought that the controller can just sit and watch but this is not true. The second consideration for ATC is expedition and that is the purpose of radar. ATC was able to run a safe, albeit slow, system before radar (it was called a 'procedural system' based on time and altitude) but now that controllers can see the positions and altitudes of all aircraft in the system they are able to speed things up.

Just as the *en route* sector controller is required to get inbound aircraft down to 13,000ft by a specified point, so the TMA outbound controller is required to get outbound aircraft up to 12,000ft by the time they leave his airspace to enter the en route sectors. The altitude specifications on the initial phases of the outbound routes ensure that the requirement for safety first is satisfied, but rigid adherence to those altitudes over long distances would be uneconomic because jet engines use more fuel at lower altitudes and could mean that aircraft are unable to reach their cruising levels by the time they leave UK airspace. This would lead to added co-ordination with the ATC systems of other countries and, perhaps, problems for them in continuing the climb to high levels.

The outbound controller will therefore be looking for an opportunity to climb his traffic above the standard altitudes as soon as possible. In a constantly changing situation he will be watching the entry point CCTV and will know whether aircraft are holding and where, and he can see those aircraft on radar with their SSR data blocks showing their altitudes. If an outbound route crosses below a holding pattern which is occupied there is little chance of climbing until clear of it. Fortunately not all outbound routes do that.

The controllers for a particular quadrant sit together at the same radar screen and each can see the other's FPS displays so each will know the other's workload and possible problems. Just as at Heathrow, they talk to each other and discuss how best to control the traffic. It may be that the outbound situation is busy but there are only a few inbounds and it will help the outbound controller if inbounds descend only to 10,000ft until clear of outbound routes. If this is agreed between the two, but only after it is agreed, the outbound controller can operate up to 9000ft until clear of inbound routes when he can clear aircraft to the top of his airspace and transfer them to en route. An early transfer can make a lot of difference to the en route controller.

Of course, if the inbound situation is the busier, that controller will need to operate down to his lowest available level so that he can safely separate his aircraft before they reach the airport holding points and he will be given priority. That sort of give and take is perfectly OK, in fact it helps to solve problems and increases the safety factor.

A little more here about standard departure routes which are officially known as Standard Instrument Departure Routes (SIDs). They are published in a document called the United Kingdom Air Pilot for the information of both pilots and controllers so that they all know precisely the procedure to be followed after take-off. They include the route defined in relation to NDBs or VORs as well as the altitudes (6000ft or lower) at which various positions must be crossed. Each SID will have a name which is usually that of a VOR en route but may be a VOR/DME fix if, for example, the position to be defined is over the sea. Thus we have SIDs named Midhurst, Sampton or Dover, among others, which have the names of en route VORs, and Hardy, Drake and Benbo which are VOR/DME positions in the English Channel. These names are what the air controller at the airport looks for when he is sorting his departure sequence.

Let us follow a SID through the various stages of a departure from Gatwick. A Britannia B767 aircraft bound for Tenerife is loaded, the doors are closed and the pilot wishes to start engines and taxi for take-off. He calls ATC on RT, 'Gatwick Delivery this is Britannia 132 requesting start-up'. There are no en route restrictions or departure delays and the planning controller replies 'Britannia 132 you are cleared to start. Runway 26. Your clearance is a Midhurst departure to Tenerife South'. (This clearance is merely a confirmation of the pilot's planned intention.)

At this stage the FPS is passed to the ground controller and the aircraft callsign and SID will appear on a CCTV on the TMA (South) suite at LATCC. When the aircraft is cleared by GMC to push-back and taxi a diagonal stroke will show on the CCTV to put the TMA outbound controller in the picture and allow him to start thinking ahead.

The FPS will be passed to the air controller as the aircraft approaches the runway holding point and he will look particularly at the aircraft type, the SID and any restrictions before instructing the pilot how to position in the queue, if there is one. When BAL

132 is cleared for take-off the diagonal stroke on the CCTV is crossed and when the controller broadcasts the take-off time this is also written on the CCTV display. The time is also fed into a computer and, almost immediately, the appropriate FPSs will be printed and distributed on all the LATCC suites which will handle the aircraft, showing the flight details and times at various points en route.

Since this is a Midhurst departure, ie, almost straight ahead (Dia 12.5), Gatwick tower will not need to retain the aircraft on its frequency and it will be transferred to TMA control within about a mile of the runway.

The pilot will follow the SID as published, and it reads like this:

	ROUTE	ALTITUDES
MIDHURST SID	After take-off	Cross
	continue straight	MID DME 10 above
	ahead to intercept	2500ft
	Midhurst VOR radial	MID DME 8 at 3000ft
	068 to Midhurst VOR,	MID VOR at 4,000ft
	to route via Airway R8	

So the routing is quite straightforward. The pilot simply continues on the runway heading until he intercepts Midhurst VOR radial 068 and flies along that *to* the VOR. He leaves MID on the R8 radial *from* the VOR. This is also published and is MID VOR R263. At the same time the pilot climbs to cross the various DME ranges at the specified altitudes. In this SID the first two altitudes ensure that the aircraft remains at least 500ft *above* the bases of different sections of controlled airspace but the third (MID VOR at 4000ft) keeps the aircraft *below* Heathrow departures which cross MID DME 11 above 5000ft climbing to 6000ft at MID.

The TMA (SW) outbound controller has been expecting BAL 132. He will also be controlling any Heathrow outbounds via MID and will be aware of any traffic under the control of, or expected by, TMA (SW) inbound. If there are no Heathrow outbounds he can clear BAL 132 to 6000ft. It there are no inbounds in the TMA he will confirm this with his opposite number and authorize climb to 12,000ft before transferring control to the en route sector. But the situation is variable and the two controllers will work together to ensure the safest and most expeditious control of all aircraft in their area.

There is one further point about departure routes. SIDs incorporate what are called Minimum Noise Routes (MNR) which apply up to 4000ft at Heathrow and 3000ft at other airports. The MNR sections are laid down not by ATC but by the Department of Transport and the Airport Authorities at Heathrow, Gatwick and Stansted or by the Airport Consultative Committee at municipal and other airports such as Luton. The idea is that after take-off aircraft follow MNRs which are designed to overfly the smallest number of built-up areas but, remembering that the routes must be aligned on VORs and NDBs and that the whole of the London area is heavily populated anyway, this can be difficult. ATC then extends these routes into the airways system and publishes the whole thing as SIDs. However, all controllers are aware that aircraft may not be vectored off a SID below the specified MNR altitudes (unless this would cause a problem). Above those altitudes they may vector and they will often do so if, for example, they wish to take an outbound aircraft behind an inbound to facilitate an earlier climb.

So that is the LTMA: a complex route structure as well as a number of holding patterns and approach control manoeuvring areas which are out of bounds to TMA controllers; but with very strict rules concerning the areas and layers of airspace within which particular controllers may operate and a sharing of workload to make the whole thing manageable.

The *en route* sectors
Just as the LTMA sectors work in a different way from approach control and approach radar so do the *en route* sectors work rather differently from the TMA. Distances are greater and speeds are higher and although aircraft transfers between TMA and *en route* sectors are at what are known as 'agreed levels' there are no such agreements between *en route* sectors, and controllers working on adjacent sectors may not even be on the same control suites (Dia 12.1 and Dia 12.2). Each transfer between *en route* sectors must, therefore, be co-ordinated by telephone at least ten minutes before the aircraft crosses the inter-sector boundary.

Some *en route* sectors are sub-divided into east and west because of the natural flow of eastbound and westbound aircraft, and here controllers will be on the same suite but will keep their aircraft in their own halves of the sector and will conform to inter-sector co-ordination procedures. So, again, every controller knows the airspace which he is responsible for controlling and the rules for transferring aircraft to another controller's airspace.

There are a lot of airways over the UK. Most of them radiate from the London TMA but others cross the UK in an east/west direction to connect the continent with Ireland and the North

Atlantic. Some will merge with others at times and in such cases they will be dual-designated so that the computer will not be confused when printing FPSs.

The purpose of an airway is to protect aircraft at the levels at which they wish to fly and these are invariably at 7000ft or above en route where the airway bases can be at about 6000ft to ensure adequate protection, but lower adjacent to the airports when climbing stubs may be required. The airways fit round and above the TMAs or other controlled airspace allocated to airports so that aircraft using the major airports can remain in controlled

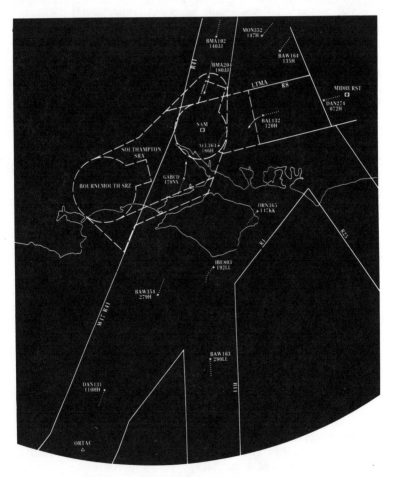

Dia 12.7. A typical Hurn sector radar display.

airspace whatever they may be doing. Airways and upper air routes extend upwards to 46,000ft.

But it was not always like this. Britain's first airway was Green One from Bristol to London in 1950. It extended only from 3000 to 11,000ft because the piston-engined aircraft of that time flew at comparatively low levels, but even so there was a great deal of opposition to it because it restricted the freedom of the air which had existed until then. As civil aviation expanded and jet aircraft came into service there was a need for more airways with higher limits and over the years the network has increased to what we see now. It seems unlikely that the route system will change significantly so the pattern of airways is probably fixed for the foreseeable future. Any additions to controlled airspace are likely to come from the expansion of regional airports which may need more protection than they have now.

Before an aircraft enters UK-controlled airspace, either from take-off or via an adjacent ATCC's airspace, a flight plan must be filed so that the aircraft is expected and FPSs can be prepared. When an aircraft takes off from an airport within the London ATCC area the take-off time is fed into the central computer and FPSs are produced at every control position at which the aircraft will be handled giving times at various points en route.

If an aircraft is entering London's airspace from any other ATCCs area, that ATCC will inform the receiving London en route sector at least ten minutes before the boundary crossing time and, again, the time will be fed into the computer and FPSs produced where required (and this includes the major airports). No-one is taken by surprise because the computer has already extracted details of the flight plans which it holds in store and produces pending FPSs about an hour in advance. These are simply up-dated when the aircraft becomes 'live'.

On receipt of the live strip the controller can expect the aircraft to call and the FPS will show the pilot's planned intention. To keep it simple let us look first at an aircraft outbound from the London TMA.

In the LTMA section we followed the flight of BAL 132 from take-off via Midhurst from Airway R8 to Tenerife. The TMA controller has climbed the aircraft to 12,000ft and transferred it to the Hurn en route sector clear of all other aircraft under TMA control. The Hurn outbound controller sees from the FPS that BAL 132 is routing from Midhurst via R8 to SAM then W17 to Ortac on the London/Brest boundary and has been allocated a cruising level of 31,000ft. Dia 12.7 shows the sort of radar picture that he might see at the time of transfer and he is responsible for that part of the sector which routes Midhurst, SAM, Ortac. The easterly part of the sector is controlled by Hurn inbound who is positioned on the same suite.

So what is it all about? We can list the aircraft under Hurn outbound control:

British Midland 102	14,000ft to Jersey
British Midland 204	18,000ft to Jersey
Monarch 352	14,700 for 39,000ft leaving UK via Hurn sector (H)
Speedbird 164	13,500 for 35,000ft leaving UK via Hurn sector (H)
Britannia 132	12,000ft allocated 31,000ft (H)
Air Europe 364	18,600 for 26,000ft (H)
Speedbird 354	27,900 for 28,000ft (H)
GABCD	17,000ft to East Midlands (NX)
Danair 131	11,000ft to Hurn (Bournemouth) (HH)

Already we can see a complication. Most of the aircraft in the Hurn sector are either inbound to or outbound from the LTMA but there are some which will route to/from Southampton/ Bournemouth while others will be to or from Midlands airports and the routes for these will lie within Hurn Outbound's sector. Some of these aircraft will have been transferred from the LTMA at agreed levels without direct co-ordination and these are MON 352, BAW 164, BAL 132, AEL 364 and BAW 354. They will all need to climb to different levels by Ortac and their times and levels notified to Brest ATCC.

BMA 102 and BMA 204 will have been co-ordinated for transfer between the crew chiefs on the Bristol and Hurn sectors, already at their cruising levels. Their times and levels must be notified to the Channel Islands Control Zone. GABCD entered the Hurn sector from the Channel Islands and will be co-ordinated into the Bristol sector at 17,000ft while DAN 131, also from the Channel Islands, will be co-ordinated into Southampton/Hurn airspace at about 5000ft for its approach and landing.

Now for the technique. The rule is that aircraft which are less than 1000ft apart vertically must be at least five miles apart horizontally. So MON 352 and BAW 164 have already been instructed to fly on parallel headings which will keep them at least five miles apart and the controller must also ensure that they will be above 19,000ft if they come within five miles of BMA 204.

BAL 132 is far enough ahead of the two climbing aircraft for them to be no problem. It is ten miles behind AEL 364 and at about the same speed so there is no problem there either. But BAL 132 has to climb above BMA 204 and GABCD and will need a continuous climb to reach its assigned level by Ortac. BAL 132 can be cleared to climb to 16,000ft, below GABCD, but if it routes via the Southampton VOR it will then be below BMA 204. The controller turns GABCD left 10° and BMA 204 right 10°. He then instructs BAL 132 to turn left to fly parallel to BMA 204 and at least five miles from its track and when all these aircraft are locked onto their headings BAL 132 can safely climb to its allocated level of 31,000ft by Ortac.

When BAL 132 has passed 19,000ft, ie, 1000ft above BMA 204, it can be cleared to continue direct to Ortac. GABCD and BMA 204 can be released to their 'own navigation' but MON 352 and BAW 164 will need to continue on parallel headings to remain clear of each other.

Meanwhile, an assistant controller has co-ordinated a level at which DAN 131 can be transferred to Southampton SRA or direct to Hurn SRZ and the aircraft will need to descend. And leaving Midhurst is DAN 274, climbing through 7200ft, still under TMA control but entering the Hurn sector.

And so on. In busy periods a continuous stream of aircraft entering or leaving the sector. Some situations are straightforward, some rather complicated but never two precisely the same. A heavily loaded long-haul aircraft will not climb as quickly as a lightly loaded short-haul. Different types of aircraft may fly at different speeds and climb at different rates. Aircraft climb better in cold weather. Strong winds may increase or decrease an aircraft's speed over the ground and there may be less or more than the average time for an aircraft to climb before it crosses the boundary. An aircraft with the wind behind it might have to be turned earlier than an aircraft flying into a headwind. With experience a controller learns to take such considerations into account before he issues instructions and all the time he scans every aircraft to ensure that it is behaving as expected. If it is not, he may have to amend a time, change a transfer level, re-plan his tactics, ask a pilot if he can expedite a climb or descent.

The airspace or sector is entirely the responsibility of the controller, but rest assured that he, or she, has spent years training for it and has been checked and examined every inch of the way. He would not be doing it if his peers had not considered that he had the ability to do so.

The inbound sectors use much the same technique, except that they start at the top and have to descend those aircraft bound for London's airports while separating them from overflights. We can look at the Lydd sector which controls two airways which are contained within the Worthing Control Area, A20 which is used by aircraft inbound to Biggin for Heathrow and to Eastwood for Gatwick, and A2 which is for aircraft for Luton and Stansted which have to descend, as well as for overflights for Scotland and the North Atlantic, or for airports north of the London area. These aircraft will have departed from France, Switzerland, Italy, Spain, North Africa and the Near East.

The transfer points from France are at Abbeville (A20) and Boulogne (A2) and aircraft from the more distant departure airports will invariably be at higher levels than those from such places as the Paris TMA. The controller has been advised by France Control of the times and levels at the transfer points and they will appear on his radar separated vertically but not necessarily horizontally. Put simply, his job is now to vector them in such a way that they are split at least five miles apart and LTMA inbounds descended to the agreed levels for transfer to the TMA in good time for the TMA controller to continue their descent to their separated holding levels. Since they are moving at speeds up to 500 mph on contact, the sector controller does not have too much time to hang about. For example, the distance from Abbeville to Biggin is only 100 miles and the TMA inbound controller will need to have the aircraft about 25 miles before Biggin. The distances Abbeville to Eastwood and Boulogne to Detling are even less.

Diagram 12.8 shows a typical radar display for the Lydd sector — bearing in mind that the radar screen is circular and that the various airways and positions are not labelled. Nor does the controller see a coastline because his interest is in airspace not topography, although he will know where it is.

This demonstrates a straightforward situation with few problems but we need to understand the SSR data blocks. Starting with the aircraft on Airway A2 routing via Detling:

Britannia 543	to Birmingham	25,800ft
Danair 297	to East Midlands Airport	28,200ft
Air France 972	North Atlantic traffic	27,600ft
Monarch 178	Luton	28,700ft
Air Europe 372	Birmingham	28,000ft
GZABC	Stansted	31,000ft

BAL 543 and DAN 297 have been co-ordinated with Clacton and Daventry sectors and are descending to 20,000ft and 22,000ft respectively before transfer in the Luton area. The same

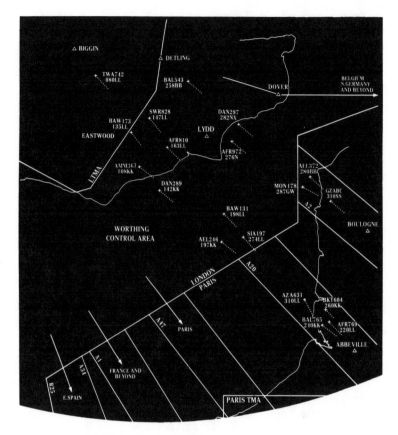

Dia 12.8. The Lydd (inbound sector) radar area.

procedure will be followed with AEL 372. AFR 972 has also been co-ordinated with Clacton and Daventry climbing to 31,000ft. He will continue north into Scottish airspace to enter the North Atlantic route structure for Montreal (see Chapter 14).

MON 178 and GZABC are bound for airports in the LTMA (North) area and will descend to an agreed level of 12,000ft by Detling for transfer without further co-ordination to TMA (NE). The agreed level is 12,000ft in this case because aircraft inbound to Lambourne from the east have an agreed level of 13,000ft and there must be no confliction on transfer.

Aircraft using Airway A20 are all inbound to either Heathrow or Gatwick (with the odd exception which may route to Midhurst for Southampton or Bournemouth) and the agreed level for transfer to TMA (SE) is 13,000ft.

We can forget TWA 742 and AMM 367. They have both been transferred to TMA and have been cleared to stack levels and, in fact, TWA 742 at 8000ft will already have been transferred to Heathrow approach for instructions.

Inbound to Biggin for Heathrow we see Speedbird 173 and Swissair 828 which are on parallel headings to maintain five miles horizontal separation in the descent. They have been instructed to maintain those headings and contact TMA to advise them. TMA will keep them on the headings until they have reached their stack levels (9000ft and 10,000ft). Air France 810 can soon be transferred to TMA and will be cleared to 11,000ft.

Speedbird 131 and Singapore Airlines 197 are no problem to each other but will be locked on to headings to keep them clear of AEL 246. Alitalia 631 is more than five miles clear of other aircraft and can be descended at any time. Air France 769, however, is in a difficult position. At 22,000ft he needs to be turned right to clear the two aircraft for Gatwick which will have to descend before he does and the controller will turn him to achieve this.

Aircraft inbound to Eastwood for Gatwick are Danair 289 which is passing 14,200ft and can be transferred to TMA for further descent and Air Europe 246 which is passing 19,700 cleared to 13,000ft and on a heading to remain clear of the two aircraft on its right. Under these circumstances SIA 197 will be cleared initially to 14,000ft and later to 13,000ft when AEL 246 has been transferred to TMA and been seen to descend further.

Just past Abbeville we know that AFR 769 has been turned right to clear Britannia 765 and Caledonian 604. Those two aircraft will also be vectored to remain clear of AFR 769 and of each other and they can then be cleared to descend to 13,000ft for the TMA, on parallel headings if necessary. AFR 769 can be descended later to be at 13,000ft by about the LTMA boundary.

That is a reasonably typical situation although, perhaps, over-simplified. There is a route inbound to Eastwood from Belgium via Lydd, another from Midhurst to Dover ánd Belgium and one from the Channel Islands to Lydd and Dover, all of which tend to complicate the issue but the idea is not to indicate the possible difficulties but rather to show the logic which governs the system.

And that is what LATCC, or any ATCC is all about. Logic, order, division of responsibility and, above all, safety.

The reader might think by now that everything in ATC happens around London or to the south. Not true. The airways to the north of London can be at least as busy as those to the south but to have discussed both north and south at the same time would have been rather complicated. So in Part 3, when we look at the airports to the north of London, we can come back to LATCC and see how what is called 'the North Bank' operates and how the north and south banks are integrated into the overall situation.

Chapter 13
Aircraft Noise

Fascinating though airports may be, and useful as they are to those who wish to travel, there are some who are not over-pleased about their activity. People who live in the vicinity of airports may suffer from the noise that aircraft are bound to make and find it an enormous problem. It is no good saying that they ought not to live there, they do and, for whatever reason, most of them cannot move away. Conversely, there is not much point in saying that an airport should not be where it is. It may well have been there before much of the development which it now affects and it would cost billions of pounds and an unthinkable amount of hassle to close it and build elsewhere. And how long before the same situation recurred?

Airports and populated areas seem not to be compatible. That is a fact of twentieth century life and will remain so for the foreseeable future and there is little that can be done about it. It is understood by the Department of Transport which has responsibility for such matters but all their expertise can only minimize the problem; they certainly cannot eliminate it.

We discussed Minimum Noise Routes in Chapter 12. These reduce the overall effect on the general population and the DoT goes further by imposing quotas and curfews on airports to restrict the numbers of aircraft using them and to ensure that they are reasonably quiet at night, but national and international economic activity (which includes tourism) provides a constant push for more aircraft and fewer restrictions. Hence the search for a third London airport as well as the expansion of regional airports.

In 1986 the DoT introduced regulations concerning actual aircraft engine noise. Some of the more modern aircraft were already meeting the restriction, others could be 'hush-kitted' but some of the older aircraft were simply scrapped. Whatever the cost, they could no longer use our airports if they were considered too noisy. These are some examples of what can and has been done to reduce the disturbance caused by aircraft, but it is difficult to see what more can be achieved unless a silent engine is ever developed.

With regard to MNRs we already know what they are and how they are incorporated into SIDs. However, such routings do require rather a lot of airspace because they may be extended to avoid some built-up areas, so they only apply to the airports within the London, Manchester and Scottish TMAs. Regional airports, which operate within much smaller zones, do not use SIDs and MNRs but they may publish preferred routes which can be varied by ATC so that they have some flexibility when separating departures from inbound aircraft. In all cases pilots are required to use the noise abatement techniques laid down for the type of aircraft. Ground running of engines is restricted to certain hours and there is a limit to the number of training flights for transport aircraft.

We cannot look at noise procedures for all airports but it might help to study Heathrow and Gatwick in some detail. Diagrams 13.1 and 13.2 show the MNRs and parts of the SIDs for both westerly and easterly operations at Heathrow. You can see that it is quite impossible to avoid all built-up areas here, particularly to the east of the airport but the situation has improved with the advent of quieter aircraft.

Those parts of the routes designated as MNRs will invariably be followed by departing aircraft but remember that they can be vectored off the SIDs when they have passed 4000 feet (Heathrow only). The shading about the MNRs indicates that aircraft tracks are affected by wind and the routes may be contained within a swathe rather than follow precise tracks. The approach paths are

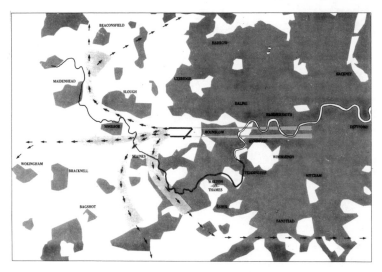

Dia 13.1. Heathrow — westerly operations.

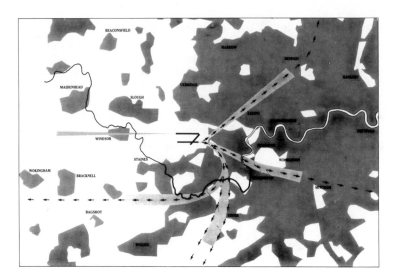

Dia 13.2. Heathrow — easterly operations.

shown as a reminder that both ends of a runway will generate noise.

Remember, too, that Heathrow has parallel runways and these will be alternated at 3 pm daily during westerly operations, although this will have little effect on noise to the west of the

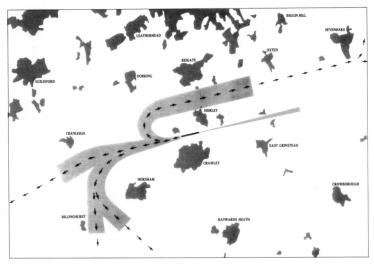

Dia 13.3. Gatwick — westerly operations.

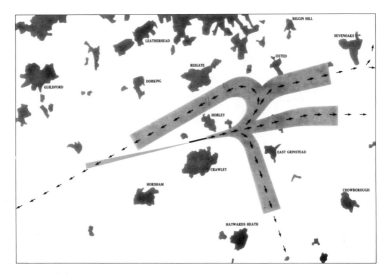

Dia 13.4. Gatwick — easterly operations.

airport because the routes from 27L and 27R merge soon after take-off. However, runway alternation does provide periods of relief for those who live on the approaches. A further point is that runways 05 and 23 at Heathrow will be used very occasionally, literally for only a few days each year, and runway 09R is also used for landing now and again. And you will not have forgotten that operations are westerly for about seventy per cent of the time.

Gatwick, shown in Diagrams 13.3 and 13.4, is surrounded by fewer built-up areas than is Heathrow and the MNRs should be reasonably effective but, even so, it is not possible to avoid every single village and some will suffer. That is unfortunate but it is inevitable.

The other airports using MNRs and SIDs are Luton and Stansted in the LTMA, Manchester and Liverpool in the MTMA and Glasgow, Edinburgh and Prestwick in the STMA. The same rules apply; routes are to be followed until aircraft are above 3000ft when they may be vectored, and that will be about eight to ten miles from the airports.

Wouldn't it be nice if there were silent aircraft engines? And motor cycles, lorries, cars . . .?

Chapter 14
Flights Across the North Atlantic

Flights between the UK and North America use a rather different ATC system from that which applies over Europe. There are no airways over the North Atlantic ('the ocean') and there are no sites on which to place VORs or other navigation aids. There are not even fixed routes because, due to the very long distances involved, pilots will wish to take advantage of the most favourable winds and weather. A variable route structure is possible because the aircraft carry their own special navigation equipment.

Not that the pilot is allowed to please himself. 'The Ocean' is controlled airspace and pilots are required to comply with strict regulations, but these are a little different from those that apply over Europe.

The Atlantic is divided into Oceanic Control Areas but we need to look at only two, those controlled by Prestwick (Scotland) and Gander (Newfoundland) which have a boundary about half way across the Ocean at 30°W and within which most UK-North America flights take place. Once clear of UK or North American airways systems, aircraft enter Oceanic airspace at points which may vary from day to day and they will remain under Oceanic control until entering the airways system on the other side.

Traffic flows across the Ocean in two phases. The eastbound flow leaves North America or the Caribbean in the evening and flies through the night to arrive in the UK in the morning. Westbound traffic leaves the UK in late morning or afternoon and arrives on the other side in the evening. (Concorde, of course, arrives in New York at an earlier local time than it leaves Heathrow.) This makes for short nights or long days for passengers but it does allow for convenient take-off and landing times.

So why do the routes change? Really it is for much the same reason why a cyclist, given a choice, would choose to cycle with the wind rather than against it — less effort and a higher speed. The same thing applies to aircraft flying across the Ocean. At the sort of altitudes at which they fly (usually above 30,000ft) the winds can be well above 100 knots and on a 3000 mile flight there can be a great saving in fuel and a big increase in speed over the surface if aircraft can fly with the wind. Dia 14.1 shows an example with high pressure over the Atlantic but remember that it could equally well be low pressure which would produce winds blowing in an anti-clockwise direction.

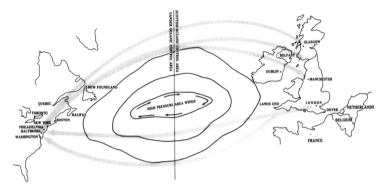

Dia 14.1. How the winds can be used to advantage on the Ocean.

Twice a day, before the start of each flow, either Gander or Prestwick will calculate the most advantageous route (or minimum cost path) and advise all those airlines and authorities who need to know. This results in aircraft leaving or entering the UK via the Ocean at points as far apart as Land's End and Stornoway or at a number of places in between. The routes are also used by aircraft to and from northern Europe and at times it is even economical for aircraft from as far south as Italy to overfly the UK to pick up Oceanic routes.

It is not possible, then, to say where North Atlantic traffic will enter or leave the UK and for the observant passenger this can provide an exercise in geography on a clear day. On outbound routes from Heathrow and Gatwick, if the English Channel can be seen on the left soon after take-off then the aircraft will probably exit via Land's End, but it could equally well cross the Severn Estuary at Bristol, fly to the left of the Welsh mountains and exit at Fishguard. These are referred to as 'Southabout Routes'. On 'northabout' days aircraft will fly north for a while and either turn left at Liverpool to cross Dublin or Belfast en route to the Ocean or will continue north to cross the Western Isles of Scotland.

Aircraft inbound to the UK will route in the opposite directions. Passengers on the way in may cross Ireland or they may be routed well clear of it to the north or south but the Ocean routes will feed into the UK system and aircraft will then be cleared to the appropriate entry point for the destination airport.

Because of the vagaries of wind and weather these long range aircraft are particularly susceptible to either late or early arrival and are a good example of the hazards of scheduling and the need for holding on some occasions. But ATC does not cause arrival delays; it simply responds to changing circumstances in the safest way possible.

Part 3

Increases in air traffic and the expansion of airports are not confined to the London area. All Midlands and Northern airports are expecting very considerable growth for at least the rest of the century and plans are in hand to cater for it. As examples of the sort of projections on which developments will be structured, Manchester handled over 7,500,000 passengers in 1986 but expects to reach twenty million by the year 2000; Leeds/Bradford had a throughput of about 750,000 in 1988 and extensive developments are in the pipeline to accommodate growth to two million. The other airports are forecasting similar increases. This part of the book looks at some of those airports, albeit with rather less ATC detail.

Airports differ in size and layout but from an ATC point of view they are all handled in the same way and this was described fully in the Chapters on Heathrow and Gatwick. To go on repeating the same old ATC procedures would be boring and tantamount to producing a catalogue so the idea here is to provide some background interest for each airport and then to show how it fits into the United Kingdom ATC system. To that end we return to LATCC after looking at the airports and we can see how the 'North Bank' operates, how the airways are integrated with the airspace allocated to the airports and how LATCC north and south banks are co-ordinated.

It can be seen that the National Air Traffic Service is truly national; and it keeps the same beady eye on both airports and ATC in all parts of the country. Your smaller (compared to Heathrow) local airport will serve you well.

For those not familiar with airports, most will have a Bureau de Change, a bank, Duty Free and Duty Paid shops, Mothers' Nursing Room, car rental, bars and buffets. There are invariably good hotels in close proximity and a night stop in a hotel to start or end a holiday can be recommended from personal experience.

Chapter 15
Manchester Airport

You may be surprised to learn that Manchester Airport has a longer history than Heathrow since it opened on its present site in 1938. It then consisted of 250 acres of grass landing area with a terminal building housing a control tower, passenger handling facilities and a restaurant. It has changed quite a lot since then.

It was originally known as Ringway (until 1955). In 1939 it was taken over by the military and became the home of the Parachute

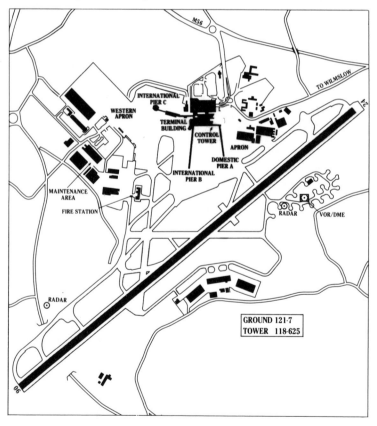

Dia 15.1. Plan of Manchester Airport.

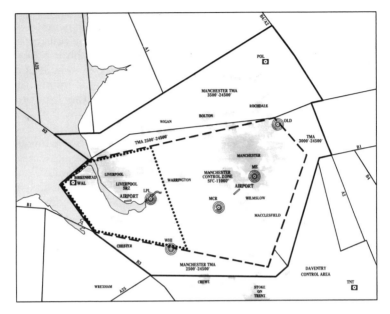

Dia 15.2. Manchester airspace.

Regiment but it returned to civil use at the end of the war and resumed its civil services in 1946.

The original runways were built by the military during their period of tenancy but the main runway (06/24) has since been lengthened. The terminal buildings were rebuilt and they came into use in 1962; there have been many other changes.

The average annual growth rate of passenger traffic through Manchester has been higher than that of most, if not all, of the other major UK and European airports over the past ten years. (It now features alongside New York, Paris and Zurich, as one of the world's top thirty international airports.) By the end of the century the throughput is projected to reach twenty million passengers per annum. Freight operations, too are modern and have enjoyed phenomenal success.

With this figure in mind Manchester Airport plc has embarked on a programme of development so great that it cannot be described in a book such as this. You name it and it is going to be enlarged or renewed or built. Airline passengers at Manchester can expect many changes and improvements to their facilities over the next few years.

Air Traffic Control and Telecommunications at Manchester are provided by the Civil Aviation Authority under contract to Manchester Airport plc. The control tower is on the top of the Terminal Building to ensure that ATCOs can see the whole of the airport; the other apparent control tower out on the apron is for the use of the airport operations staff who control the disposition of aircraft, etc.

The airport has a single runway nearly two miles long and 150 feet wide (Dia 15.1). It has been strengthened to take the big jets, it has ILS at both ends so that aircraft can operate in all weathers and it has the appropriate aerodrome and approach lighting.

Manchester operates within its own block of controlled airspace (Dia 15.2) which consists of a fairly large control zone from ground level up to 11,000ft surrounded by a control area, known as the Manchester Terminal Control Area (MTMA), which has a variable base outside the zone so that aircraft can climb safely into the airways system which radiates in all directions from the MTMA. We shall look more closely at the MTMA later; at the moment we need to consider only the Manchester and Liverpool arrival and departure routes (Dia 15.3 and 15.4). One point to note is that Liverpool has a Special Rules Zone within the

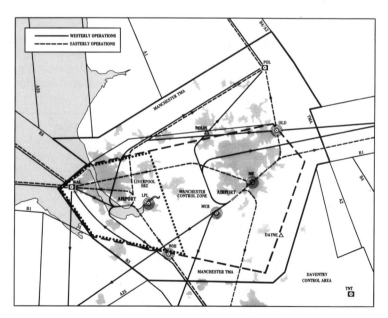

Dia 15.3. Manchester and Liverpool outbound routes.

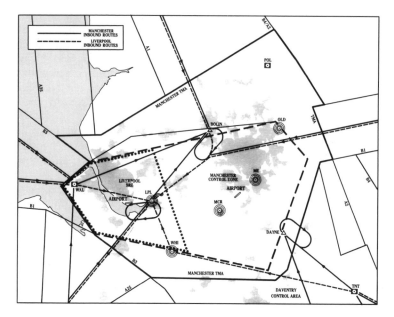

Dia 15.4. Manchester and Liverpool inbound routes.

confines of the Manchester Control Zone but it only goes up to 1500 feet. Manchester has the airspace above that.

The control tower has two controllers ('Tower' we know about from our look at other airports). They are responsible for aircraft arriving and departing on the single runway, for liaising with approach radar to ensure that the gaps in the landing stream are adequate for the various types of departing aircraft and maintaining safety above all other considerations. Just as at other airports, aircraft follow SIDs after take-off and minimum departure spacings are laid down and must be adhered to.

Some aircraft will have been allocated departure slots so that they will fit into an organized flow entering foreign airspace. Those aircraft must depart on time or the slot will be lost and it could be hours before another one can be allocated. The controller has to take this very important consideration into account and give priority to such aircraft when necessary (see Chapter 11 — Flow Control).

There is no GMP controller at Manchester, although there will surely have to be one at some time as operations increase. At the moment planning and start-ups are the responsibility of 'Manchester Ground' who also has the normal task of controlling aircraft taxiing to and from the runway or being towed between the piers and the maintenance area. He is in radio contact with all vehicles on the manoeuvring area as well as with working parties carrying out essential maintenance on the airport. He clears aircraft to push back from the piers and co-ordinates everything that moves outside the runway. Ground controllers do not actually have eyes in the back of their heads but they sometimes feel they should have.

The tower equipment is standard. Teleprinters to produce the Flight Progress Strips we all know about, an aerodrome lighting panel, ground radar, clocks set to GMT, anemometers and so on. Expert assistance is also provided by a support staff who are fully trained in ATC procedures. We have now looked at a number of airports and, really, the principles are always the same even though the airport layouts are different. Method, organization and safety in accordance with strict regulations are what an airport is all about, so all airports have a common standard.

Even so, not all airports can operate in quite the same way and Manchester is rather different in its approach control. It has an approach control unit just as at any other airport such as Gatwick but the controllers here operate alongside what is, in effect, a remoted sector of LATCC. This unit is known as the Manchester Sub-Centre and its responsibilities are to the Manchester TMA and the surrounding airways rather than to Manchester Airport direct. However, let us forget the MTMA at the moment (we will come back to it in a later chapter) and look at the way that Manchester Approach operates.

The staffing is currently a No 1 and No 2 Director, but further traffic growth will inevitably lead to a need for a third controller. There are two main entry points at positions named Dayne and Bolin (Dia 15.4). These are VOR/DME positions and if aircraft are required to hold, they will do so here in the same way that aircraft hold at Gatwick.

No 1 Director is the direct link with, and is located in the same room as, the en route control. He will accept releases in respect of traffic landing at Manchester at separated levels via the two holding points, and display the information on his flight progress board. He will identify the aircraft on his radar screen and assess distances to run, taking aircraft speeds into account, so that he can decide on an action plan and set up a likely landing sequence.

Can he vector them beyond the holding points and into a landing stream or must some enter the holding pattern? If they do need to enter the holding pattern, they must continue to be assigned separated levels. However, if they can be vectored without delay, when they are clear of all other aircraft they can begin descent from their stack levels. Should they be required to hold, the Director will control the stack and descend aircraft as levels below them become vacant.

When aircraft are clear of the stacks, have begun their descent and have been sequenced into a landing order, they are handed over to the No 2 Director for the fine tuning. He liaises with the Tower Controller and as he passes the landing order, is advised of the number and types of aircraft waiting to depart, and agrees with the Tower Controller the gaps required in the landing stream. A typical approach and landing stream is shown in the chapter on Heathrow.

One further consideration. Dia 15.3 shows that some inbound routes to Liverpool Airport enter the TMA via Bolin. Depending upon the runways in use at the two airports, it will be necessary sometimes for the Liverpool arrivals to be co-ordinated with Manchester and to be transferred to Manchester Approach, to be separated and descended before being passed on to Liverpool Approach.

Chapter 16
Liverpool Airport

Like so many other airports Liverpool (Speke) began its life in the early 1930s as a grass field. During the war it was taken over by the RAF who constructed runways. However, in 1966 a new runway was opened (7500ft) to accommodate the jet aircraft that were then coming into service. For some years Liverpool operated a north and a south airfield, a most unusual set-up, but in 1982 all operations were transferred to the south airfield. In 1986 a new passenger terminal and car park were opened and various other improvements were made.

The wartime history of Liverpool is most interesting. It housed fighter squadrons which flew in defence of Liverpool and other areas of the north-west and Midlands, bomber squadrons operating over Europe, various types of flying training units and some squadrons of the Fleet Air Arm. Aircraft for Allied Forces overseas were flown into Speke, dismantled, crated and shipped

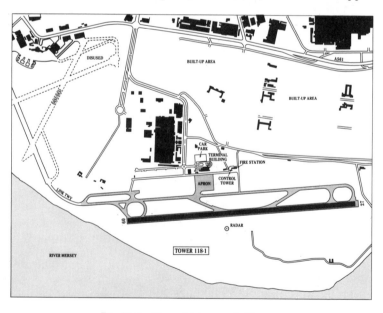

Dia 16.1. Plan of Liverpool Airport.

abroad from the Port of Liverpool. Aircraft from the USA came into the port in crates and were then re-assembled at Speke and flown out to operational squadrons. And while all this was going on the Rootes Group was producing Blenheims, Beaufighters and those lovely old Halifax bombers. This was a very busy airfield and there were frequently over 200 aircraft on site at one time.

The post-war history of the airport was a bit gloomy and some of the independent airlines using Liverpool ceased to operate. Regional airports generally had to struggle but things are now looking bright. Liverpool is no exception.

Following the new runway, terminal building and control tower, Liverpool acquired a new apron and a fire station as well as a large Royal Mail Sorting Office which handles over fifteen per cent of the country's first class mail five nights a week. A new cargo centre is being built next to the passenger terminal and several organizations are expected to start aviation-related businesses on the airport.

The ATC organization here is standard. Tower and approach are manned by licensed ATCOs employed under contract and they use the same procedures as Manchester, Gatwick or any other airport.

The airport layout is shown in Dia 16.1 and you will see that this was very well planned. At each end of the runway there is an escape loop, which means simply that if a pilot wants to delay his take-off for some reason (to double-check an instrument, perhaps) he can taxi into the loop and landing aircraft can continue without being obstructed. At the middle of the runway there are angled turn-offs (called high speed turn-offs) which allow some aircraft to leave the runway at a good taxiing speed instead of having to slow right down before making a 90° turn.

The tower controller has a good view of the runway, taxiway, apron and approaches. Aircraft departing for airways follow SIDs and after take-off they will be transferred to the Manchester TMA (the SID routes are shown with Manchester routes). If departures are not using airways but wish to clear the Liverpool zone at low level they will be co-ordinated with airways departures, and separation will be established before transfer of control.

Some Liverpool departures will be subject to flow control and, when this is so, DFR at LATCC will issue a departure slot time which must be adhered to. Single-runway operation was dealt with more fully when we looked at Gatwick. It is just the same here. Approach control is also much the same: it is all a matter of scale. The inbound routes are shown under Manchester, and Liverpool approach and radar work closely with both Manchester

TMA and Manchester approach control. Some 'inbound releases' from Manchester TMA to Liverpool will be at fixed positions and altitudes (eg, Wallasey VOR at 4000ft), after which Liverpool approach will assume control of the aircraft while it is being sequenced onto the approach to the runway when it will be transferred to aerodrome control in the tower. Other aircraft might have to be separated from Manchester arrivals by Manchester approach control before Liverpool inbounds can be transferred and this will be done by direct controller to controller 'radar handover'. If aircraft are required to hold they will do so on Liverpool NDB.

So standards are the same as at Heathrow. ATC procedures are based on the same principles for all airports. Liverpool is AOK.

Chapter 17
Birmingham International Airport

From the ATC point of view, most of the growth in aviation before about 1980 seemed to be taking place at Heathrow and Gatwick. The other airports were just pottering along, some bigger or busier than others, but none very significant.

Then came the Airports' Big Bang! It seemed almost suddenly that more traffic was being generated from regional airports and we became aware of new building and updating of facilities because of new investment and new ideas. The regionals went into business with a determination to be a part of, or even perhaps to some extent a catalyst for, economic growth in their regions. We have seen what is happening at Manchester. Birmingham was not to be left behind.

The airport opened in 1939 just in time to be requisitioned by the Air Ministry who used it to train pilots throughout the war. Since it was also used as a flight testing and delivery base for Lancaster and Stirling bombers, two runways were built during that time. Civil operations re-started in 1946. The terminal building was extended in 1961 and the main runway was lengthened in 1967. The opening of the National Exhibition Centre in 1971 provided a spur for major development and passenger levels continued to rise but it was not until 1981 that building started on the new Birmingham International Airport which opened in 1984.

In 1987 a new company, Birmingham International Airport plc, was formed to manage the airport. The company is wholly owned by the seven Metropolitan District Councils in the area and their policy is clearly to aim for everything that an airport should be in the airline passenger and air cargo business. Safety can be left to the ATC and telecommunications staff who are provided by the CAA.

On the east side of the airport is the very impressive and spacious terminal building with restaurants, shops and other services. This is only a short stroll from the car park or ninety seconds on the MAGLEV transit system from Birmingham International BR station.

The control tower is on the south-west side of the airport overlooking the freight area and Freeport with a good view of the whole of the airport operation. There are two runways; the main one, 15/33 has a length of 7400ft with the other, 06/24, being 4310ft long. They are both 150ft wide (Dia 17.1). The main runway can take all aircraft up to jumbo size but 06/24 is reserved for General Aviation aircraft and they are the private, business, executive, club and training types. Since both runways can be used at the same time it means that GA aircraft can operate with the minimum of interference to the larger aircraft which have to use the main runway — so all traffic gets faster treatment.

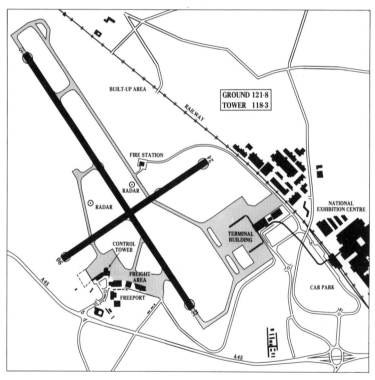

Dia 17.1. Plan of Birmingham Airport.

Birmingham has its own control zone within a radius of eight nautical miles from the airport with the Birmingham SRA stubs lying to the north-west and south-east of the zone in line with the airways (A1 and B3) which overlie the airport (Dia 17.2). As ever, the zone extends upwards from ground level for the

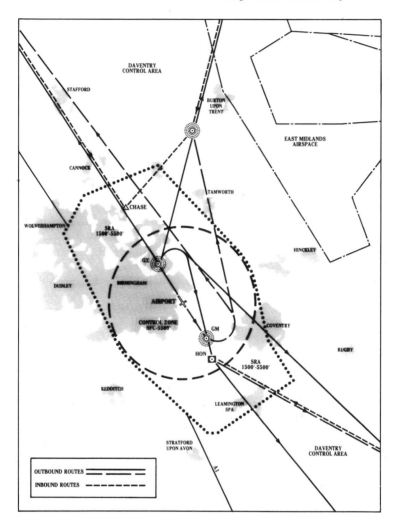

Dia 17.2. Birmingham airspace and routes.

protection of all airport traffic while, in this case, the SRA has a base of 1500ft to protect aircraft either on the approach or climbing out. They both have an upper limit of 5500ft but, since the airways have a base of 4500ft, this nicely marries up the two types of airspace and gives Birmingham aircraft full protection.

We have previously looked at airport single runway operation, most fully at Gatwick, and there really is nothing different about Birmingham. Yes, there is a second, crossing, runway but that does not affect the issue. The majority of aircraft using Runway 06/24 will not be entering the airways system and they will be issued with ATC clearances to keep them clear of airways departures and arrivals until they leave the zone. There is nothing unusual about this: all airports have traffic which does not arrive or depart via airways. What these aircraft cannot do is enter the zone without permission. Nor can they take off and leave the zone, or transit any part of it, without permission and they are organized and integrated by ATC through clearances to proceed according to circumstances.

The airways departure procedure for Birmingham is a little different from the airports that we have looked at previously in that Birmingham does not have SIDs. Aircraft here follow Outbound Standard Departure Routes as shown in Dia 17.2 and each aircraft has to be cleared (accepted) by its en route controller before it can take off. In the case of departures for any route south of Brimingham that will be the LATCC Daventry sector but aircraft to the north will enter Manchester's airspace and will need a clearance from MTMA. So Birmingham tower has direct telephone lines to the crew chiefs at both places.

Inbound routes are also shown in Dia 17.2. Birmingham is not multi-directional in its departure and approach phases so we see a simpler pattern. The drawing shows three positions in line with the main runway. 'GM' and 'GX' are NDBs, Chase is a VOR/DME position. The 'GM' (Golf Mike) is used as a holding facility for aircraft from the south via LATCC Daventry sector while aircraft from the north are directed by MTMA to Chase where they may be held if necessary. Both these holding positions are in Birmingham airspace so Birmingham controllers are in charge. The crew chiefs will ring Birmingham approach for clearance to enter the SRA as well as an entry level.

Not all aircraft get to the holding facilities. Approach radar controllers will always try to 'snatch' inbound aircraft to fit them into the approach pattern early and that frequently happens here. Whichever way it is done, we are back to the familiar system of radar directing, radar sequencing and liaison with the Air controller. Just like any other airport.

Chapter 18
East Midlands International Airport

East Midlands Airport was built in the early 1960s on the site of an abandoned RAF aerodrome known as Castle Donington. (Interestingly, the airport still uses 'Castle Don' as its radio callsign.) There was not much of the old aerodrome that was usable so, in effect, East Midlands was the first all-new civil airport to have been commissioned for many years. The need for an airport had been shown, the site was available, the location (within a triangle formed by Derby, Leicester and Nottingham) was more than suitable and road and rail communications were good and getting better.

The airport opened in 1965 under the authority of the East Midlands International Airport Joint Committee which was financed and controlled jointly by Derbyshire County Council, Leicestershire County Council, Nottinghamshire County Council and Nottingham City Council. On 1 April 1987, the airport became a limited company under the Airports Act. The four Councils are now the shareholders. The aim of the Committee was to provide all the services that those in its catchment area could have hoped for, and this it has done to a quite remarkable degree. The airport now has scheduled services to London Heathrow, Amsterdam, Paris and Dublin, all with world-wide connections, as well as to Belfast, Glasgow, Aberdeen, Edinburgh, Jersey and Guernsey. It has taken a good slice of the Inclusive Tour holiday market and it has shown rapid increases in its cargo and Post Office mail operations.

Three fast-growing airlines, British Midland Airways, Air Bridge Carriers and Orion Airways chose East Midlands as their bases, as did Donington Aviation, which is an important air taxi company. Field Aviation Services maintain, service, repair and 'fit-out' aircraft of many types at this airport and there are a number of other aviation-related businesses here. Quite an empire. And growing.

It goes without saying that an airport such as this will have the most up-to-date facilities, not only for passenger and freight handling but for ATC as well. There is a modern control tower, a recently updated radar and ILS and lighting on a 7500ft runway. Overall, a very efficient airport but, apart from personal pride in the job, there are pressures for a top class service at all airports: the airlines are very quick to point out what they see as problems. This is seldom necessary but their suggestions can be useful and they are always listened to.

As you can see in Dia 18.1, this is a single runway airport. We have previously looked at the way that a runway is controlled and it could be boring to repeat that for every airport. The chapter on Gatwick explains the system and the others are much the same.

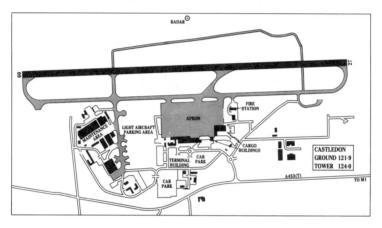

Dia 18.1. Plan of East Midlands Airport.

Approach and radar control also operate on the same principles as elsewhere; only the types of holding facility and their positions relative to the runway will be different. Dia 18.2 shows the regulated airspace allocated to East Midlands and the inbound and outbound routes for the airport.

EMA airspace is quite complex. The zone extends upwards from the surface but has two different upper levels. The area has three different lower levels and it, too, has two different upper levels. It seems better to say simply that it is all designed to provide protected passage to/from airways and, although arrivals are officially via the NDB 'EMW', the shape of the airspace enables radar to arrange early transfers from en route sectors so that separation can be provided sooner and landings expedited.

The ATC procedures for departures are a little different from Birmingham's in that all departures must be cleared out by MTMA but aircraft will be transferred to airways control when

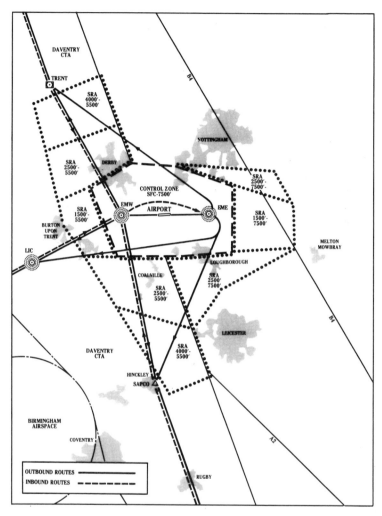

Dia 18.2. East Midlands airspace and routes.

they leave EMA airspace and Castle Don radar will provide any separation required up to that stage.

Arrivals will need clearance into EMA airspace and the particular area controller will contact East Midlands approach control for a co-ordinated arrival level. Where there is a conflict between an inbound and an outbound the two controllers concerned will agree which of them is responsible for resolving the situation. This, of course, is where radar comes into its own.

Controllers can see the radar returns from aircraft and will know when it is safe to drop or climb one through the level of another. They have to be three miles apart before that can be done but the ATCO can turn both aircraft onto (or lock both aircraft onto) headings to achieve the lateral separation which will enable him to clear aircraft safely to climb or descend.

Note that in the smaller control zones and SRAs which do not have separated inbound and outbound routes, as at Heathrow, radar controllers frequently have to control departing aircraft as well as arrivals so that separation is assured at all times. It is all highly organized and very disciplined.

STOP PRESS. In November 1988 it was reported that Orion Airways was being taken over by Britannia Airways, Britain's second largest airline.

Chapter 19
Leeds/Bradford Airport

In common with all other UK airports owned by local authorities and having a turnover in excess of £1,000,000, Leeds/Bradford was required by the Airports Act 1986 to form itself into a Limited Company. Leeds/Bradford Airport Ltd is owned and operated by the five Districts of West Yorkshire. Leeds and Bradford each own forty per cent of the company whilst Wakefield, Kirklees and Calderdale share the remaining twenty per cent in equal parts.

The airport provides scheduled and charter services for passengers and freight in a catchment area which covers most of the Yorkshire and Humberside region with a population of nearly five million. It has a long history dating back to 1931 when the operators were the Yorkshire Aeroplane Club whose interests were in flying, training and general club activities. The first scheduled air service, by North Eastern Airways Ltd, was in 1935. Between then and the war a small number of other airlines operated out of the airport but only to UK destinations and, as was the standard of the time, with not too much reliability.

Leeds/Bradford was taken over by the RAF during the war, when it was called Yeadon. It was used as a flying training school and an aircraft maintenance unit but, more importantly, a factory was built to the north of the airport and used by A. V. Roe to produce some 4500 Anson, Lancaster, Lincoln and York aircraft. Such aircraft required runways and these were built at that time.

Between the years 1948 and 1953 the airport was operated by the Ministry of Civil Aviation but they then withdrew, and so did the few civil services that had moved in. For a few years the situation was hardly dynamic but the Leeds/Bradford Airport Joint Committee took over in 1959 and things began to change. A new Airport Manager (later Airport Director) was appointed. The runway was extended, airfield lighting and ILS were installed, the aircraft parking apron was extended and passenger accommodation was enlarged. A new passenger terminal building was built later; it opened in 1968.

All this was still not enough for the new generation of jet aircraft and in 1980 the airport authority was granted planning permission to extend the main runway, 14/32, by 2000ft to 7400ft, and to extend the terminal area and freight handling facilities.

The initial costs were met by the ratepayers but the Airport Committee's decision seems to have been the right one since the airport now shows useful profits after meeting all outgoings including debt charges.

Regional airports do not happen by accident; they need proper research before decisions can be made. The then Joint Committee had commissioned a report in 1972 and the conclusion was that West Yorkshire and Humberside needed an airport. Hence the extensions and improvements to Leeds/Bradford. What did they lead to?

This is not a major airport nor was it intended to be. So far as the public is concerned, it has three main functions. It provides a number of scheduled services for business travellers to such destinations as Aberdeen, Amsterdam, Belfast, Cardiff, Dublin, Edinburgh, Glasgow, the Isle of Man, the Channel Islands, London and Paris — and even one B747 service a week to Toronto. Some of these flights are feeder services which connect at major airports like Heathrow and Amsterdam with intercontinental flights, while holiday charter flights also use Leeds/Bradford. In addition the airport caters for cargo handling, air taxi operations, executive flights, a flying club and an aircraft sales and maintenance company.

The aerodrome itself is not unusual in any way. Like Birmingham it has a main and a subsidiary runway and GA aircraft can be separated from the bigger aircraft unless strong winds demand that they all use the longer runway. Conversely, some of the airline aircraft can use the shorter runway if there are strong easterly or westerly winds. It must be stressed, though, that airport noise regulations require that the long runway should be used wherever possible (Dia 19.1).

The same rules and regulations apply here as elsewhere. Standard separations must be maintained, departure slots are critical, safety is paramount. The ATCOs here are Non-State but they pass the same examinations and have the same qualifications as ATCOs employed by NATS. In fact NATS sometimes sends its trainee controllers here to gain experience.

The Leeds/Bradford SRZ and SRA fit neatly into a corner of the airways system adjacent to the north-east corner of the MTMA (Dia 19.2). The zone looks slightly lopsided but regulated airspace is always tailored to the actual needs of the airport and, at this one, airways arrivals and departures will invariably operate on the airways side, ie, to the west or south. Because Leeds/Bradford airspace is not under an airway the upper level of both the zone and the SRA is 8500ft. This ensures that aircraft can

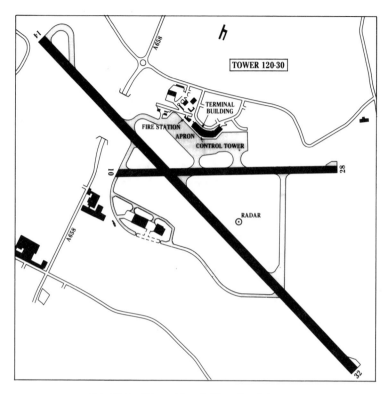

Dia 19.1. Plan of Leeds/Bradford Airport.

climb into or leave the MTMA at reasonable levels and are not squeezed down.

Dia 19.2 shows the geographical limits of the two types of airspace and you will see that the zone extends upwards from the surface (SFC) while the SRA bases are 2500ft and 3000ft. Again this is tailoring the airspace to the requirement, so the zone protects aircraft down to ground level and the area protects climbing and descending aircraft, leaving the airspace below it free for General Aviation.

The routes to and from the airways system are also shown in Dia 19.2. You will notice two things. First, most airways departures route via the VOR at Polehill which is within MTMA airspace, and most of the inbound routes also transit the MTMA. Second, there is some conflict between inbound and outbound routes in the Leeds/Bradford SRA and SRZ. In the first case the MTMA controllers will keep Leeds/Bradford traffic clear of all Manchester

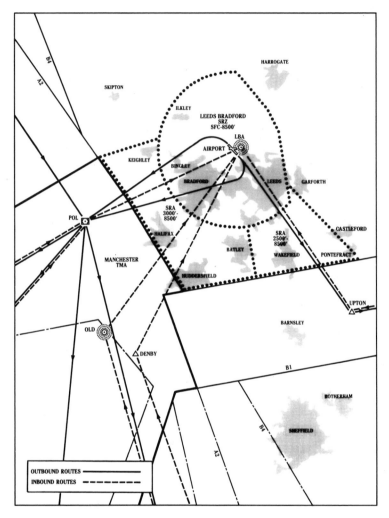

Dia 19.2. Leeds/Bradford airspace and routes.

inbound and outbound aircraft using a combination of procedural control and radar. That means that L/B inbounds are cleared only to levels above Manchester traffic until it can be seen on radar that aircraft are at least five miles clear of each other when L/B inbounds can continue their descent. Outbound aircraft from L/B will only be cleared to levels 1000ft below any Manchester or L/B inbound traffic until, again, it can be seen that any conflicts have been resolved.

Within Leeds/Bradford airspace the same rules apply. Agreement is reached with Manchester on the levels to which aircraft can be cleared in or out and radar will ensure aircraft safety when they need to climb or descend through each other's levels.

It is the same old ATC story. Each controller has his own area of responsibility, be it in the air or on the ground. He or she is responsible for separation and safety within that area and for ensuring that aircraft passed on to another controller are separated and will maintain that separation on transfer. Leeds/Bradford is the same as Gatwick in this respect, although with fewer movements and fewer controllers.

A valid point about regional airports. A potential operator wishing to run an airport, or its own ATC service, has first to obtain CAA approval. This may be granted subject to the airport meeting specified licensing criteria but this approval requires annual renewal which is preceded by a full inspection of all operational aspects by a team of CAA specialists. An ATC service can only be operated by personnel with the relevant CAA licences validated for that particular airport and these, too, have to be renewed annually, both medically and professionally. Just like pilots.

Chapter 20
Newcastle International Airport

When the airways system was first established over the UK in the 1950s the main north/south axis was Prestwick — London — Paris. This route crossed the industrial north and Midlands but the airports there at the time did not generate much traffic. Most of the aircraft using that original airway were either from Scotland or from the North Atlantic routes. North-east airports were way out on their own and very much off-route.

As airports have developed and traffic has increased, more airways have been established around the original north/south route, and east to west airways through the Manchester and London areas have also been set up. But Newcastle and Teesside are still out there, well clear of the airways system. As they got busier there became a pressing need to provide some form of protection for their aircraft while they were in transit between the airports and the airways system.

The routes were not busy enough to be given airways status but a long-range radar service became available from a joint military/civil radar station to the north of Newcastle. A 'Radar Advisory Service Area' (RASA) was established within which all aircraft

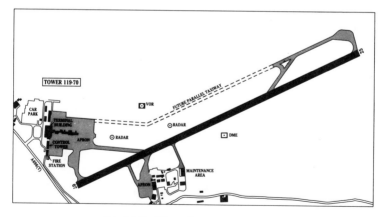

Dia 20.1. Plan of Newcastle Airport.

were asked to participate and radar routes were set up between Polehill VOR in the MTMA and Newcastle and Teesside airports as well as from Dean Cross VOR up by the Scottish Border. We shall just look at the Polehill route which is not direct because there is some very busy airspace between Polehill and the airports. Aircraft go north from Polehill until they are west of the airports and then direct, always receiving a radar service. For aircraft leaving or joining airways at Polehill the RASA controllers and the airways controllers co-ordinate by telephone.

Newcastle International Airport itself is owned and operated by a private limited company, the total share capital of which is held by seven local councils. (The Regionals used to be known as Municipal Airports.) It is a modern, thriving airport but the management is not resting on its laurels and it has forward-looking plans for continuous updating and refurbishment. Airports do experience a lot of wear and tear in all areas and the authorities must always look to the future.

Like many of the Regionals, Newcastle started as a grass aerodrome in the 1930s and was taken over by the Air Ministry 'for the duration'. But this airport did not get the benefit of runways built for the RAF and the only legacy of their occupation was a sort of control tower (probably called the 'Watch Office') which might well have been built by Heath-Robinson himself! It was not until the 1950s that it started to come together as a real airport and the latter half of the 1960s before it acquired a new terminal and a runway suitable for modern aircraft.

Newcastle International has come a long way since then. It now offers scheduled services to both London's airports as well as to Paris, Amsterdam and Dublin for international connections. There are also services to Toronto, Oslo, Bergen, Stavanger, Jersey, Guernsey, Belfast, Aberdeen, Humberside, Norwich and Manchester. Holidaymakers have a choice of over forty destinations and all types of aircraft up to B747 and DC10 can be seen at the airport.

The single runway has a length of 7650ft (Dia 20.1) and both ends are equipped with ILS and full aerodrome and approach lighting. The control tower is very 'with it', the usual set-up with the VCR on top housing the aerodrome controllers with the approach and radar controllers on a lower floor. All the equipment is up-to-date and there is a bunch of happy ATCOs to man it.

There is one slight difference in the aerodrome configuration in that the runway does not have a full-length parallel taxiway. So, as at Luton, some aircraft may have to back-track before take-off or after landing but the loops at each end of the runway make this a quite straightforward operation. The construction of a parallel taxiway has been approved to meet future demands.

And so to the actual ATC operation, and it can only be said again that all airports operate in much the same way. Within the system an airport is a sector and each ATCO controls a sub-sector. The air controller's responsibilities here are the same as for the air controller at Gatwick: organize departing aircraft in such a way that there are no unnecessary delays and that separation is provided between departing and arriving aircraft. Ensure that aircraft with departure slots allocated by LATCC take-off on time. Keep an eye on weather and runway conditions. Liaise with No 2 Director so that the landing aircraft spacing is right for the types of departures. Check how and when radar is needed for aircraft after take-off to ensure their separation from arrivals and to control them on climb-out. Conform to standard procedures so that everyone involved understands what is happening.

Approach control is a little different. Newcastle regulated airspace (Dia 20.2) is not adjacent to airways so aircraft arrive or depart via the RASA. At the Newcastle end co-ordination and

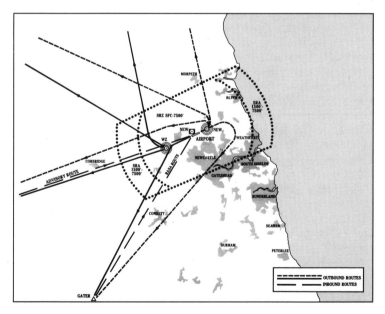

Dia 20.2. Newcastle Airspace and routes.

transfer of control will be between Newcastle radar, who will control the initial climb or the intermediate descent, and the RASA controller who will continue the climb for outbounds or begin the descent for inbounds and provide en route control. We already know that the RASA and airways controllers co-ordinate levels at Polehill (and Dean Cross).

There is more yet. The RASA has a lower level of 10,000ft but you can see that Newcastle's airspace only goes up to 7500ft. Within this gap and, in fact, for a radius of forty miles from the airport (excluding the airspace of other airports), Newcastle radar participates in a Lower Airspace Radar Service (LARS) which covers much of the country outside Controlled Airspace and offers a radar service to civil or military aircraft. Newcastle was the first civil airport to be involved in LARS.

The primary function of Newcastle approach and radar, though, is to accept inbound aircraft from whatever source, to keep them separated, to hold them if necessary on one of the NDBs, to sort and sequence them and to position them on the ILS approach at the correct intervals for landing. Air Traffic Control is very standardized. If procedures are the same for all airports, and they are, then pilots will know what to expect and the system will operate in an orderly, and safer way.

Chapter 21
LATCC North Bank

In Chapter 12 we looked at the general organization of the London Air Traffic Control Centre and its modus operandi to the south. We saw how outbound aircraft are transferred from the airports to the TMA controllers, from them to the en route sector controllers and then on to adjacent ATCCs. Inbound aircraft are accepted from adjacent ATCCs by the en route sectors, descended to agreed levels for transfer to TMA controllers, further cleared by them to stack levels and then transferred to approach control at the airports for sequencing onto the various runways.

You will remember the complex pattern of inbound and outbound routes across and around the LTMA but that vertical separation is built into those routes until they have crossed. Radar controllers who can 'see' the aircraft on their screens clear aircraft to climb or descend beyond those agreed levels.

We know, too, that some aircraft overfly at higher levels and will pass from one sector to another, sometimes through three or more sectors, and that when flight plans are activated for any aircraft entering UK airspace Flight Progress Strips are produced for all sectors which will handle the aircraft. Co-ordination must be effected by sector crew chiefs before an aircraft can enter another sector.

One consideration in such a co-ordination is that two airways or routes may cross a common point in different directions, one east/west and one north/south. For example, an aircraft from the Dover to the Daventry sector will cross east or westbound routes in the Clacton sector. When this happens then 'standard separation' must be built in to any co-ordination. Aircraft at the same levels must be not less than ten minutes apart at the point of crossing. Less than ten minutes, they must be at different levels at least 1000ft apart (but 2000ft if either is above 29,000ft).

The principles of separation remain the same wherever aircraft fly. Standard separation can be vertical or timed where routes cross, longitudinal (time or distance) when aircraft follow the same route, or lateral in the case of holding patterns against routes or other holding patterns and that means a minimum distance apart. Radar separation is at least five miles for aircraft which have less than 1000ft vertical separation. These are ICAO standards and they can only be reduced in certain circumstances such as radar control in a TMA or landing stream.

These separations are engraved on ATCO's hearts and implanted into their brains, as are the limits of the controlled airspace in which they operate. We know about the separations; now we can consider the airspace which is relevant to those aircraft we have discussed in Chapters 15 to 20.

First some orientation between geography and controlled airspace from the Scottish ATCC border down to the London area, a distance of about 270 miles (Dia 21.1). We cannot show too much detail on a drawing of this size but enough to show the relationship between main towns and cities, the airways system and the controlled and special rules airspace allocated to the airports. Additional detail can be seen in the more localized drawings.

It is time to say a little more about the MTMA and you will see that its area of responsibility (shaded on the drawing) extends well beyond the TMA boundaries. The unit which controls this airspace works on one of the lower floors of Manchester tower and it is known as the Manchester Sub-Centre. It is, in effect, a distant sector of LATCC and, in fact, this sub-centre is divided into three sectors of its own, MTMA (NE), MTMA (SE) and MTMA (IOM). Manchester approach control works alongside them.

So why a sub-centre? Well, this is a complex area. Remember the number of airports that have aircraft which transit the MTMA — and we have not even looked at the Isle of Man, Belfast, Blackpool and Carlisle. It was considered more efficient to have area specialists at Manchester to control all aircraft (including those overflying the Manchester area) within a defined area and up to 15,000ft. Aircraft above that altitude are controlled by LATCC en route sectors. Those descending for the MTMA area are controlled by LATCC en route down to 16,000ft before handover to MTMA. Aircraft leaving the MTMA airspace will be transferred to LATCC en route when they cross either the vertical or lateral boundaries of the TMA and are clear of all other aircraft under MTMA control.

In Dia 21.1 we can see how the route system works. Since the original ten-mile-wide airway, a number of others have been added which run either alongside or at an angle across the original one and we now have a system between London and Manchester which can be as much as fifty miles wide. None of it is wasted. There are two main streams, one running north on the east side of the airways, the other running south on the west side. Tributaries allow traffic to leave the main streams for the airports or to join the main streams on departure. Within the streams some aircraft

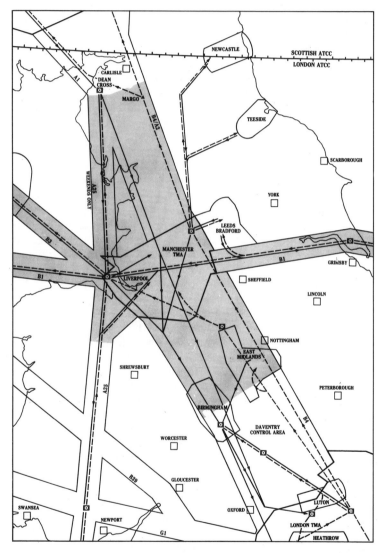

Dia 21.1. Orientation of airspace and routes north of London to Scottish TMA.

may be climbing while others descend or some aircraft may be faster than others and will overtake and wish to climb or descend through. Five miles separation is required for such clearances and a lot of airspace is needed during busy periods. The Daventry sector is split into east and west sub-sectors so each controller will have only half of the total width of airspace.

The traffic density can vary quite a lot. When the east-bound flow off the North Atlantic in the early morning is via Scotland and Ireland (See Chapter 14) and it happens at the same time as the south-bound rush from Scotland and the regional airports to London, it becomes so busy that flow control might have to be imposed. Aircraft already airborne have priority so the delays then would be suffered by departures from within the UK. If NAT departures are via the Daventry sector then again departure flow control might have to be laid on. But all in the interests of safety because this can be the busiest airways sector in Europe and must not be allowed to go over the top.

When we looked at LATCC in Chapter 12 we saw in transit through south bank's airspace two aircraft descending en route for Birmingham, another for East Midlands and an Air France aircraft climbing on its way to Scottish airspace to join a North Atlantic track. They had all been co-ordinated from Dover, through Clacton and into the Daventry East sector.

In Dia 21.1 we can follow the routes these aircraft would take to the north of the LTMA and see how they are joined by aircraft from the London area. Since they are northbound they will stay on the eastern side of the sector when they can, but Birmingham aircraft must leave the stream by about Luton and cross to the other side of the Daventry Control Area where they will meet the southbound flow. However, they were already descending when we last saw them and that descent will be continued so that they will be below the southbounds when they are handed over to Birmingham approach. The aircraft for East Midlands will be vectored clear of and below all other aircraft in the stream before transfer to EMA approach. The Air France will continue to climb to its assigned level of 31,000ft and cross Polehill and Scottish airspace for its North Atlantic track.

But that is not the only route on to the Ocean. Some aircraft may fly north to Trent, just north of EMA airspace, and then cross Manchester TMA to route either B1 or B3. Other aircraft from Europe could cross the east coast on B1 near Grimsby either inbound to Manchester, Liverpool or Leeds/Bradford or over-flying for Belfast, the Isle of Man, Dublin or a North Atlantic route. Diagram 12.2 shows that B1, B3 and the airways north of

Manchester are in the Polehill and Irish Sea sectors, so any aircraft flying from the London area to the north of Manchester requires a co-ordination. And, all the time, Manchester is the controlling authority for any aircraft at 15,000ft or below while a LATCC sector controls aircraft above that. It is all very three-dimensional but the controllers concerned know precisely who is responsible for what.

Aircraft from Scotland, Belfast or Dublin (either Domestic or Oceanic) converge in the Manchester area. Some overfly to the east while others descend to land in the area. Let us look at those overflying towards the London area via the Daventry West sector which are joined by southbound departures from all the Midlands and Northern airports.

First a small diversion. Because the Manchester to London airway can get so very busy, another airway, A25, was established to reduce the load on the Daventry West sector. A25 runs from about Liverpool and then south past Cardiff and Exeter, crossing the coast at Brixham for the Channel Islands, Spain, Portugal and the Canaries and it is used by aircraft from Manchester and points north. This is the aerial equivalent of a relief road and was a very welcome addition to the airways system. As a point of interest, aircraft using this route are controlled by LATCC south bank's Bristol sector because that sector also controls G1 which is crossed by A25 to the north of Cardiff.

Back to Daventry West. Overflights from Polehill and the Irish Sea are co-ordinated into the sector by the respective crew chiefs. As an example of the sort of levels used in those sectors, shuttle services from Scotland via Polehill sector can be as high as 37,000ft while aircraft off the Ocean might be even higher. Aircraft from the Irish Sea (B1 and B3) can be at much the same levels but they must all be separated on transfer and the Daventry crew chief ensures that they are.

Not all aircraft wish to fly at high levels so the medium levels will be occupied by these, as well as by aircraft descending to land in the Manchester area.

As we come south of Manchester we have the overflights at 16,000ft or above and these are now joined by aircraft departing the Manchester area and climbing out of the top of the MTMA and later by aircraft leaving the MTMA box at 15,000ft or below. Departures from East Midlands or Birmigham now join the stream. Many of the departures bound for Europe which have joined the stream since Manchester will want to climb. Certainly the LTMA controllers will want them above their airspace which extends up to 13,000ft.

Meanwhile, among the medium- and high-level aircraft we may have some which will overfly to the west of London bound for France, Switzerland or Italy and these will wish to maintain their levels. But most will be inbound to the London area (Bovingdon for Heathrow and Willo for Gatwick) and these must be separated from the overflights and descended to 13,000ft before they reach the LTMA.

It is all rather complicated. Jet aircraft use less fuel at high levels. Those up there want to stay as long as they can, departures want to get up there as soon as possible and you may be surprised to learn that even aircraft from Manchester to London will climb to levels between 17,000ft and 23,000ft only to descend again within minutes.

So we have a mix of climbing and descending aircraft and the rule is that aircraft must be at least five miles apart when levels are crossed. To ensure this separation, controllers have to instruct pilots to fly on headings which will keep them separated until they reach their cruising levels and/or are clear of all other aircraft. This needs a lot of airspace but remember that the Daventry East controller may be having his or her own problems with the northbound stream so both controllers have to remain within their own sectors.

Meanwhile, those old FPSs constantly appear for new aircraft or are discarded when aircraft have left the sector. Because the controller cannot remember every instruction to every aircraft he must write those instructions on the strips. Controllers use red ink but, since co-ordinations are also written on the strips, crew chiefs use green ink. It is said at LATCC that, away from the ops room, you can distinguish sector controllers from crew chiefs by the ink stains on their fingers. Anyone with red fingers but sporting a green pen is assumed to be ambitious.

That is about it for LATCC North Bank. We have not looked at the Clacton sector or LTMA (NE) and LTMA (NW) but there are no significant differences between them and the TMA and en route sectors that we have seen. No more pictures of radar screens, either, but each sector will see its own area on the screen with a bit of overlap and it is hardly possible to show the radar for every sector.

LATCC is a very large organization and it employs some extremely hard-working, dedicated people, and not only ATCOs. It is very highly organized, very disciplined and very demanding.

Part 4

Now we go north of the border but not to talk about haggis and bagpipes. In the world of aviation we still see the same ATC procedures, the same professionalism, the same discipline and, as ever, dedicated staff who take the job very seriously indeed. The intention here is to show how Scottish airports and airspace play their part in the overall ATC system. Not in great detail because we have already seen how an ATCC works and how major airports operate, but enough to show the passenger or the interested layman what goes on and to add to the picture for the UK.

Chapter 22
Glasgow Airport

The airport for Glasgow used to be at Renfrew but it was re-located at Abbotsinch in May 1966. Renfrew had become too small and could not be expanded. In 1960 a decision had been taken by Glasgow Corporation that Abbotsinch should be developed as the new airport for Glasgow: in 1963 the then owners, the Royal Navy, de-commissioned the ship and departed leaving the way clear for re-development and rebuilding to civil airport standards.

The change from one aerodrome to another was an event that will never be forgotten by those who were involved. On the evening of 1 May 1966 Renfrew handled its last flight. All through the night fleets of vehicles ferried to Abbotsinch equipment belonging to airlines, Air Traffic Control, HM Customs and Immigration, caterers, shops and a bank (and many others), all of which had to be in position for the first flight arrival at 0800 hours next morning. And they did it! Many of the staff had never worked at an airport before and it is recalled that even the Airport Director and Deputy Director were driving tractors and trailers on that first day to get everything where it was supposed to be. But it all went well for aircraft and passengers and the standards achieved during that period are claimed by Glasgow airport to have been their hallmark ever since.

The airport was taken over by the British Airports Authority in 1975. In 1986 the BAA became a public limited company; Glasgow Airport Limited (the present owners) became a subsidiary and so began a new and important stage in the development of the airport. In September 1986 the board of BAA plc approved a £110m plan to further improve standards and increase business. The users here have much to look forward to.

What about now? Well, Glasgow airport is not just a facility, it has become big business and is in competition with other airports. This competition makes them all try harder and Glasgow won't be left behind. Hence the £110m for development. The airport offers a wide range of services. General cargo, newspapers, first class mail, Datapost and express deliveries, much of which is carried in the holds of passenger aircraft, although some airlines specialise in freight operations, holiday flights by most of the charter airlines, and scheduled services between places as far apart as Vancouver to Berlin and Reykjavik to Pula. On some days there are nearly 25 flights to Heathrow and Gatwick with a flight time of about 75 minutes and providing airline connections worldwide. There are additional flights to Stansted plus flights to many other UK and European airports.

Passenger facilities are good and getting better. ATC equipment is constantly updated at very great expense so that Glasgow's Air Traffic Control system is a world leader. The main runways are fully equipped with the latest ILS and approach lighting for reduced visibility landings so that bad weather delays are kept to a minimum.

There are two runways. The main runway, 05/23, is 8720ft long and is suitable for all types of aircraft. The secondary runway is 10/28 and this has a length of 3540ft so it is used only by medium to light aircraft (Dia 22.1).

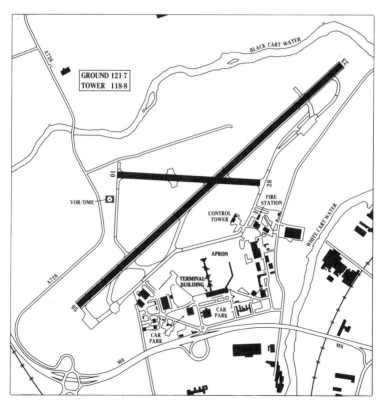

Dia 22.1. Plan of Glasgow Airport.

The control tower operates in the same way as any other control tower. Because the aerodrome is smaller and less complex than, say, Heathrow, a separate GMP controller is not necessary here so start-up clearances and SIDs are issued by the ground controller who is also responsible for all aircraft, vehicles and persons on the manoeuvring area. When GMC has resolved any problems with departing aircraft he, or she, can transfer them to the air controller as they approach the runway holding points. And, of course, when aircraft clear the runway after take-off, the air controller transfers them to ground control.

Aircraft departing Glasgow for airways follow SIDs which bear such names as Lomon, Foyle, Clyde, Helbo, Perth, Dean Cross, Talla and Turnberry. These names tell controllers the route the aircraft will follow after take-off and the air controller will use them to sort the aircraft into the safest departure sequence. For example, from runway 23 Dean Cross and Talla SIDs will turn left after take-off while Clyde and Helbo SIDs will turn right. If the controller can alternate these SIDs, the alternating aircraft will turn away from each other after take-off. Where this is not possible a minimum time separation must be imposed and this will vary with the types of aircraft. An aircraft not going 'airways' but leaving the zone at low level will be given a direction of turn after take-off, an altitude to fly and a track or position to leave the zone. This is virtually the same as a SID so the principle remains the same and the same type of separation is applied.

As elsewhere, the air controller is responsible for the safety of all aircraft using the runway. He must also ensure that those aircraft with slot times get away on time. We have been through the procedures before (at Gatwick) and those who wish to recap can refer to it. To go through it all again for every separate airport could be boring, and airports are anything but that. Ground control was dealt with very fully in the chapter on Heathrow.

Approach control is carried out in a new (1987) control room which is equipped with the most up-to-date radar consoles and communications systems. Controllers here co-ordinate and accept aircraft from Scottish Centre (SCATCC) and we will look at that unit in the next chapter. Diagran 23.1 shows the procedure for aircraft from LATCC airspace to Glasgow and Edinburgh. Such aircraft are at levels up to 28,000ft when they are transferred to SCATCC control at a position called MARGO just south of the SCATCC/LATCC boundary.

SCATCC controllers will separate Glasgow inbounds from all other traffic, turn them towards Glasgow and descend them. At about forty miles from Glasgow they will be transferred to

Glasgow approach control who will clear them for further descent. Should there be inbound delays and aircraft are required to hold they will be cleared to different levels at the VOR/DME holding point at Fenik where the stack will be controlled by the approach controller, while the No 1 Director will instruct aircraft to leave the stack and begin the approach as required.

If there are no delays, Glasgow radar will vector the aircraft so that they form, in effect, a mobile queue, speeds will be adjusted, aircraft will be cleared to approach altitudes and the queue will be vectored round onto the ILS for the runway in use at the correct intervals for landing. Different approach patterns for different airports but basically the same method as described for Heathrow.

Chapter 23
Scottish Air Traffic Control Centre (SCATCC)
Oceanic Area Control Centre (OACC)

SCATCC is located at Prestwick on the west coast of Scotland. Its area of responsibility covers some 137,000 square miles extending from the LATCC boundary in the south to 61°N near the Faroe Islands, east to the boundaries of the Norwegian and Danish areas and west to the boundary of the Oceanic Control Area which we looked at in Chapter 13.

The Centre itself is manned by highly trained NATS specialists (men and women) who work with the most up-to-date radar and communications equipment in a very pleasant control room that also houses their support staff and all the necessary computer input positions and teleprinters. One of the computer input devices at SCATCC activates flight plan information held in the LATCC computer thus providing, automatically, essential information for their colleagues in the south.

SCATCC is not as big as LATCC but the methods of operation are much the same except that every sector controller has an executive controller who carries out the functions of the crew chief at LATCC and also organizes controller to controller radar handovers so that agreed levels are not used here.

In Dia 23.1 we see the hub of the system, the Scottish TMA, with Airways B4, A1 and A2 which connect Scotland to England and the Continent, B2 which runs from Prestwick to Dublin and Belfast, and B22 Glasgow to Aberdeen. Also shown are a number of Advisory Routes which are used between the TMA and various Highlands and Islands airports, all of which have their SIDs, plus two 'N' routes which connect the UK Airways System to North Atlantic tracks.

Not shown are the internal routes between Scottish airports, the inbound/outbound routes for Aberdeen and the SIDs for easterly operations and the H and I routes. These would make the drawing too complex.

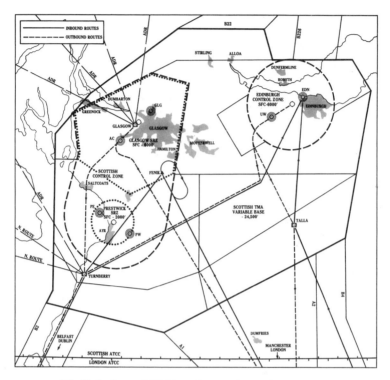

Dia 23.1. Scottish TMA and routes (westerly operations).

During peak periods, Scottish Centre can generate a lot of traffic, most of which is going south. When these peaks coincide with northabout flows off the Atlantic routes and all this combined traffic flies south to join the departures from Midlands airports it can all be more than the LATCC Daventry sector can handle safely. When this happens flow control is imposed by the DFR at LATCC and Scottish Centre is given a rate at which traffic can be accepted by LATCC. SCATCC will then issue departure slots for Scottish airports. This will not happen every day but it is most likely to happen in the early morning.

SCATCC is divided into sectors, of course, which vary in size according to the density of traffic. In the TMA the Talla and Galloway sectors divide the responsibilities between the eastern and western parts and there are three en route sectors which look after the airspace around and above the TMA.

We have already been through the airways control procedure. An ATCO is responsible for an airway or part of it. Before any aircraft leaves the sector for another it must be co-ordinated and accepted, and so on. For transfers between SCATCC and LATCC the procedure is just the same.

Within the TMA the rules are equally firm. No-one operates in isolation. No controller may operate in another controller's airspace, all transfers must be co-ordinated in advance. The zones within the TMA are the province of the airport controllers who are responsible for separation between aircraft in the zones.

There are a number of holding points for the three airports in the STMA. Aircraft required to hold at Prestwick will do so on the NDBs on the approaches to the runways or on the Turnberry VOR. Edinburgh has two NDBs, one on the approach to each runway. Inbound aircraft will be routed initially by TMA towards the NDBs at the approach side of the runway, at separated levels of course, and will be held there if necessary. Glasgow has a similar arrangement of NDBs in addition to the VOR/DME holding point at Fenik so the radar approach pattern is not as straightforward as might have been thought.

The whole set-up is different in layout from the LTMA but is operated in much the same basic way. If SCATCC is not described in detail it is because it was all done for LATCC and (I am sure they will agree) it is just another Centre, with radar screens, VDUs, telephones, keyboards, teleprinters, computer inputs and the ubiquitous Flight Progress Strips. And, let us not forget, some very dedicated and hard-working people who will not let you down.

There are some more of the same in the Oceanic Area Control Centre which is also located at Prestwick. This is a completely different unit whose job is to control aircraft which are en route between Europe and North America. Its eastern boundary is well to the west of the UK and it has no responsibilities for aircraft flying over Britain. However, the Oceanic system is not dealt with here. Aircraft cross the Atlantic from or to many airports in the UK but the majority are from Heathrow or Gatwick and, so, it was decided to include a description of Oceanic control in Part 2 under the heading 'Flights across the North Atlantic'.

Part 5

This section of the book has nothing to do with Air Traffic Control. It is about how to get to airports, where to park, airline users and flight enquiry telephone numbers. All the information here was provided by the airports and it is given more or less in the form in which it appears in their passenger information booklets — hence the differences in layout.

Lists of airline users and telephone numbers were correct as at December 1988 but it must be pointed out that these may change at any time for a number of reasons. Airlines are sometimes bought out, services may be withdrawn or introduced at particular airports, new handling agents may take over, and so on. And it must be stressed that these are same-day flight enquiry telephone numbers which must not be used for general enquiries, reservations or even forecasts of what might happen tomorrow or next week. When flow control is in operation, to the extent that it makes the national news, the advice from the airlines will always be to turn up on time so these telephone numbers should not be used for such enquiries.

Airline flight prefixes are given as both two and three-figure codes because airlines and airports will come into line with ATC in the use of prefixes but it is not known precisely when this will be. Some have already changed.

No information is given for Stansted because the rate of change there is so rapid that any information could be misleading.

A word of warning. Do not leave cars or luggage unattended at airports and do not enter restricted areas. The regulations are for security or safety reasons and must be observed at all times.

S1 Heathrow

If you are thinking of driving your own car into Heathrow the advice from Heathrow Airport Ltd is simply 'Please don't'. The airport can get very busy and adverse weather or delayed flights can cause severe congestion on airport roads and make driving 'far from enjoyable'. Those who have experienced such problems would probably use much stronger language.

Many people have the option of using other means of transport, buses, coaches or underground trains. Whichever, the first essential is to know the terminal you need because Terminals 1, 2 and 3 are located in the central area while T4 is on the south side of the airport. There is no pedestrian subway link between the Central Terminal Area and T4.

The following list shows airlines terminal by terminal, their flight prefixes and flight enquiry telephone numbers.

TERMINAL 1

Aer Lingus	EI/EIN	(01) 745 7017
Air UK	UK/UKA	(01) 745 7017
British Airways — UK Shuttle and European flights (not Paris and Amsterdam)	BA/BAW	(01) 759 2525
British Midland	BD/BMA	(01) 745 7321
Brymon Airways	BC/BRY	(01) 759 1818
Cyprus Airways	CY/CYP	(01) 759 1818
Dan-Air	DA/DAN	(01) 759 1818
El Al	LY/ELY	(01) 759 9771
Icelandair	FI/ICE	(01) 759 1818
Manx Airlines	JE/MNX	(01) 745 7321
Sabena Belgian Airlines	SN/SAB	(01) 759 1818
South African Airways	SA/SAA	(01) 759 1818

TERMINAL 2

Aeroflot Soviet Airlines	SU/AFL	(01) 759 1818
Air Algerie	AH/DAH	(01) 750 3000
Air France	AF/AFR	(01) 759 2311
Alitalia	AZ/AZA	(01) 725 7807
Austrian Airlines	OS/AUA	(01) 745 7114
Balkan-Bulgarian Airlines	LZ/LAZ	(01) 759 1818
CSA Czechoslovak Airlines	OK/CSA	(01) 759 1818
Finnair	AY/FIN	(01) 759 1818
Iberia	IB/IBE	(01) 897 7941
JAT Yugoslav Airlines	JU/JAT	(01) 759 1818

LOT Polish Airlines	LO/LOT	(01) 759 1818
Lufthansa	LH/DLH	(01) 750 3000
Luxair	LG/LGL	(01) 745 4255
Malev Hungarian Airlines	MA/MAH	(01) 759 1818
Olympic Airways	OA/OAL	(01) 759 1818
Royal Air Maroc	AT/RAM	(01) 759 2311
SAS	SK/SAS	(01) 745 7576
Swissair	SR/SWR	(01) 745 7191
TAP Air Portugal	TP/TAP	(01) 759 1818
TAROM Romanian	RO/ROT	(01) 759 1818
Tunis Air	TU/TAR	(01) 759 2311
Turkish Airlines	TK/THY	(01) 759 1818

TERMINAL 3

Air Canada	AC/ACA	(01) 759 2331
Air-India	AI/AIL	(01) 897 6311
Air Mauritius	MK/MAU	(01) 897 1331
Bangladesh Biman	BG/BBC	(01) 759 1818
BWIA International	BW/BWA	(01) 897 1331
Egyptair	MS/MSR	(01) 759 1520
Ethiopian Airlines	ET/ETH	(01) 759 1818
Ghana Airways	GH/GHA	(01) 759 1818
Gulf Air	GF/GFA	(01) 897 0402
Iran Air	IR/IRA	(01) 745 7222
Iraqi Airways	IA/IAW	(01) 759 1818
Japan Airlines	JL/JAL	(01) 759 9880
Kenya Airways	KQ/KQA	(01) 745 7362
Kuwait Airways	KU/KAC	(01) 745 7772
Malaysian Airline System	MH/MAS	(01) 759 1818
Middle East Airlines	ME/MEA	(01) 759 9211
Nigeria Airways	WT/NGA	(01) 759 1818
Pakistan International Airlines	PK/PIA	(01) 759 2544
Pan American World Airways	PA/PAA	(01) 409 0688
Qantas	QF/QFA	(01) 400 1010
Royal Jordanian Airlines	RJ/RJA	(01) 759 2331
Saudia Saudi Arabian Airlines	SV/SVA	(01) 745 4373
Singapore Airlines	SQ/SIA	(01) 759 1818
Sudan Airways	SD/SUD	(01) 759 1818
Thai International	TG/THA	(01) 897 1331
Trans World Airlines	TW/TWA	(01) 759 5352
VARIG Brazilian Airlines	RG/VRG	(01) 897 1331
VIASA Venezuelan Airlines	VA/VIA	(01) 897 1331
Zambia Airways	QZ/ZAC	(01) 725 0747

TERMINAL 4

Air Malta	KM/AMC	(01) 745 4133
British Airways — Intercontinental flights including Concorde, Paris and Amsterdam flights	BA/BAW	(01) 759 2525
KLM Royal Dutch Airlines	KL/KLM	(01) 750 9820
NLM City Hopper	HN/NLM	(01) 750 9820

Now we know where we are let us look first at the public transport system beginning with the underground railway which is connected to the Greater London underground railway network. The airport has two separate stations, both on the Piccadilly line, using a single direction loop (Dia S1.1) with trains calling first at

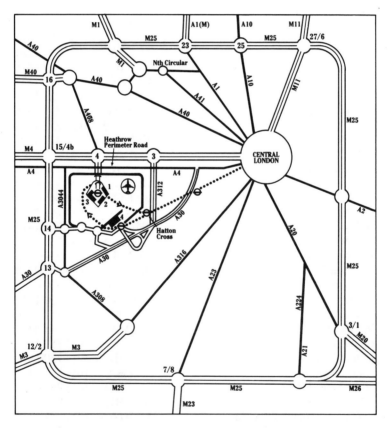

Dia S1.1. London/Heathrow Airport road access.

Hatton Cross before continuing to T4, then T1, 2 and 3, back to Hatton Cross and thence to Central London.

By interchanging, the underground line links the airport with British Rail terminal stations and, through them, to the countrywide rail service. Average journey time from Heathrow to Piccadilly Circus is 47 minutes, to King's Cross 55 minutes and to Liverpool Street (change at Holborn) 61 minutes. Trains run every three minutes at peak times extending to about every seven minutes off-peak and Sundays.

To make life easy, Terminals 1, 2 and 3 are connected to the station by an enclosed pedestrian subway system which has moving walkways wide enough for baggage trolleys. If you are leaving the airport the trolleys may be taken up to the ticket barrier at T1, 2 and 3 and up to the platform entrance at T4.

But the underground is only part of the public transport system. There is a quite amazing list of bus and coach services which connect the airport not only with various parts of London but with places as far apart as Penzance (six a day), Bristol (fifteen), Bournemouth (twenty), Swansea (sixteen), Leeds (six), Liverpool (five), Glasgow (three) and the Victoria Coach Station (31) from which coaches operate to all parts of the country. So if you are going to Heathrow it is worth checking. If you are leaving by public transport there are information desks located in each terminal.

Some bus and coach services terminate at the Central Bus Station which is linked via the subways to Terminals 1, 2 and 3. These services will show on their destination indicators a letter which relates to a particular bus stop in the central area. Other services call at the terminals and these are shown by the terminal numbers. It should be pointed out that there is a bus stop 'T' in the Central Bus Station, not to be confused with a terminal number.

However, if you decide to drive to the airport, check again which terminal you require. Terminals 1, 2 and 3 in Heathrow's Central Terminal Area are accessed via the tunnel from the A4 Bath Road or the M4 (Junction 4 then M4 Spur). For Terminal 4, drivers from London should take the A30 or leave the M4 at Junction 3 and follow the signs direct to Terminal 4. Drivers from all other areas are advised to take the M25 leaving the motorway at Junction 14, the designated exit for Terminal 4, and follow signs on the Southern Perimeter Road (Diagram S1.1).

If you are dropping a passenger you may do so and unload baggage outside each terminal but no waiting is permitted. Do not leave your car unattended outside the terminals as it may (and

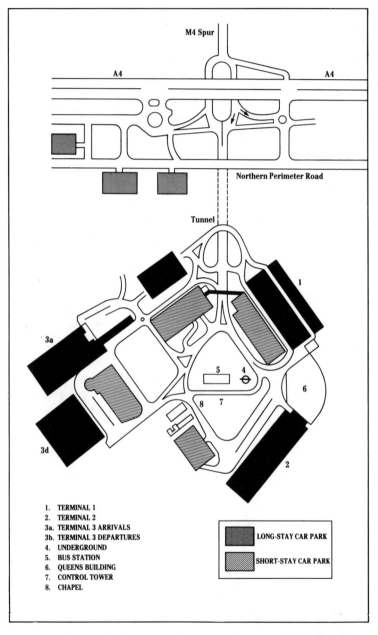

Dia S1.2. London/Heathrow Airport parking terminals 1, 2 and 3.

probably will) be removed by the police and it will cost you an awful lot of money to get it back. Having delivered a passenger, if you then want to see him or her off, or if you are going to pick someone up, you should park in a short stay car park.

For stays of over three hours it is cheaper to stay in the long stay car parks which are intended for people such as business travellers. These long stay car parks are well signposted at all the main airport entrances and are sited on the Northern Perimeter Road for Terminals 1, 2 and 3 and on the Southern Perimeter Road for Terminal 4. They are all served by free and frequent courtesy coaches to and from the respective terminals. Car parks are shown in diagrams S1.2 and S1.3.

A word now for those who wish to visit Heathrow and just gaze at aircraft. This may be done from the spectators' viewing area in the roof gardens of Terminal 2 where there is a refreshment buffet

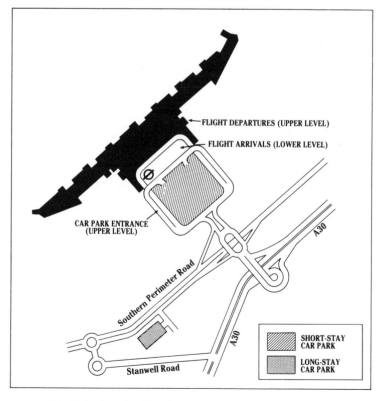

Dia S1.3. London/Heathrow Airport parking terminal 4.

and a souvenir and book shop. It is open daily except Christmas and Boxing Days from 0930 to 1800 hours in the summer and 0830 to 1630 hours in the winter. However, in certain circumstances the area may be closed and it is suggested that you telephone (01) 745 7115 before your visit.

The public transport services are ideal for spectators. The Central Bus Station is connected by footbridge to the Queen's Building which provides access to the viewing area. Spectators driving to the airport are advised to use the long stay car parks for Terminals 1, 2 and 3 where they can park for up to twelve hours for just £2.30, take the free bus service to Terminal 1 and walk to the Queen's Building.

Spectators are not permitted in the terminal buildings. And no dogs!

S2 Gatwick

Gatwick is a little less complicated than Heathrow because it has only two terminals, North and South. All the road and rail travel links are to one side of the airport with easy access to the terminals and all you have to do is follow the signs. You will need to know which terminal you want but this is quite straightforward. 'Which Terminal?' information is displayed throughout the terminals but for those who wish to plan ahead, the airlines are listed below.

NORTH TERMINAL
Air 2000	AMM
Air France	AF/AFR
Air New Zealand	TE/ANZ
Air Zimbabwe	UM/AZW
British Airways	BA/BAW
British Island Airways	KD/BIA
Caledonian Airways	KT/BKT
Connectair	AX/CAX
Emirates Airlines	EK/UAE
GB Airways	GT/GBL
Monarch Airlines	OM/MON
SAS Scandinavian	SK/SAS

SOUTH TERMINAL
Adria Airways	ADR
Aer Lingus	EI/EIN
Aeroflot	SU/AFL

Aeromaritime	QK/QKL
Aigle Azur	ZI/AAF
Air Atlantis	AIA
Air Canada	AC/ACA
Air Europa	UX/AEA
Air Europe	AE/AEL
Air Holland	AHD
Air Lanka	UL/ALK
Air Malta (Charter)	KMC
Air Malta (Scheduled)	KM/AMC
Air Seychelles	HM/SEY
Air UK	UK/UKA
Air Vendee	VM/AVD
Air Yugoslavia	YRG
Alitalia	AZ/AZA
Amber Air	DMD
American Airlines	AA/AAL
American Trans Air	AMT
Arkia	IZ/AIZ
ATI	BM/ATI
Austrian Airlines	OS/AUA
Austrian Charter	OB/AAT
Aviaco	AO/AYC
Aviogenex	JJ/AGX
Balair	BB/BBB
Balkan Bulgarian	LZ/LAZ
Baltic Airlines	HOT
Braathens SAFE	BU/BRA
Brit Air	DB/BZH
Britannia Airways	BY/BAL
Brymon Airways	BC/BRY
CAAC (China)	CA/CCA
Cal-Air International	EN/CAI
Cameroon Airlines	UY/UYC
Canafrica	NCR
Capital Airlines	BZ/CPA
Cathay Pacific	CX/CPX
Continental Airlines	CO/COA
Corse Air	SS/CSS
CTA	CTA
Cyprus Airways	CY/CYP
Dan-Air	DA/DAN
Delta Airlines	DL/DAL
Euroair	EZ/URO

Garuda	GA/GIA
Guernsey Airlines	GE/GER
Hispania Lineas	HSL
Interflug	IF/IFL
JAT	JU/JAT
Korean Air	KE/KAL
KAR Air	KR/KAR
KLM	KL/KLM
LAC	CN/LIC
Lufthansa	LH/DLH
Maersk Air	DM/DMA
Minerve	IW/MRV
Nationair Canada	NX/NXA
NLM City Hopper	HN/NLM
Northwest Airlines	NW/NWA
Norway Airlines	NOS
Oasis	AAN
Paramount	PAT
Philippine Airlines	PR/PAL
Piedmont Airlines	PI/PAI
Royal Air Maroc	AT/RAM
Ryan Air	FR/RYR
Scanair	DK/VKG
Spanair	NR/SPP
Sterling	NB/SAW
Swissair	SR/SWR
Tarom	RO/ROT
TAT	IJ/TAT
Toros Airlines	TAU
Transavia	HV/TRA
TWA	TW/TWA
Tunis Air	TU/TAR
Uganda Airlines	QU/UGA
Universair	UN/UNA
Virgin Atlantic	VS/VIR
Viva Airlines	VIV
Wardair Canada	WD/WDA
Worldways Canada	WG/WWC
Yemenia (Yemen)	IY/IYE

If you find yourself in the wrong terminal, no problem. Take the transit to the other one.

If you wish to make a same-day flight enquiry, remember to quote the flight number and destination or departure airport.

FLIGHT ENQUIRIES

Aer Lingus	0293 502671
Air Europe	0293 502790
Air France	01-759 1818
Air New Zealand	01-759 1818
Air Zimbabwe	01-759 1818
American Airlines	0293 502671
Britannia Airways	0293 502790
British Airways	01-759 2525
Caledonian Airways	0293 567100
Cathay Pacific Airways	0293 567711
Connectair	01-759 1818
Dan Air Services	0293 502671
Delta Airlines	0293 502671
Emirates Airlines	01-759 1818
Garuda Indonesia Airways	0293 502671
GB Airways	01-759 1818
Monarch Airlines	0293 502671
NLM City Hopper	0293 567711
Northwest Airlines	0293 502671
Philippine Airlines	0293 567711
SAS Scandinavian Airlines System	01-759 1818
Virgin Atlantic Airways	0293 502671
Wardair Canada	0293 502790
All other airlines	0293 31299

The lists of airline users should please the aircraft spotters and other spectators who are most welcome at Gatwick. There is a spectators' gallery on the roof of South Terminal with access from the arrivals concourse; there is a very small charge and the gallery has a buffet and Skyshop. If you wish to check the availability of the gallery the telephone number is 0293 503843.

There is a wide choice of public transport to and from Gatwick. The airport's British Rail station is part of Gatwick's South Terminal with escalators and lifts to and from platforms. A 'Gatwick Express' operates between the airport and London Victoria station every fifteen minutes during the day and hourly at night and there are two trains every hour between Gatwick and London Bridge. There are also services to south coast stations as well as to others on BR's Network South East with, of course, connections and interchanges to the whole of the BR system.

Local buses run frequently between Gatwick, Crawley and Horley and there are direct express coach services between

Gatwick, Heathrow and Luton as well as many major towns. Services to most parts of Britain can be joined at Victoria coach station in central London (half a mile from Victoria rail station). There is a bus and coach information desk on each arrivals concourse and information and tickets for most services are available in the coach station waiting room which is on the ground floor of South Terminal. Take the lift.

Car parking is no problem. Decide which terminal you want and whether long or short stay and just follow the signs from the M23 Junction 9 or the A23. Free bus services are provided between terminals and long stay car parks. Covered walkways connect terminals to short stay car parks. Passengers may be set down on the upper road level at either terminal. Drivers dropping or meeting passengers should park in the appropriate short stay car park before going to the concourse. (NB: Private cars may not wait on the airport's road system. Sussex police operate a tow-away system on behalf of Gatwick Airport Limited for cars left unattended and the retrieval charge would make your eyes water just as much as at Heathrow.)

For how to get to Gatwick and where to park see Dias S2.1 and S2.2.

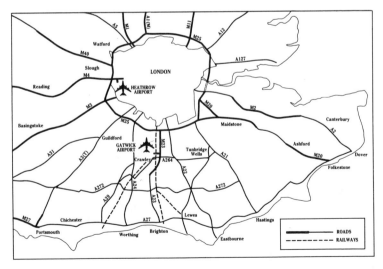

Dia S2.1. London/Gatwick Airport Road Access.

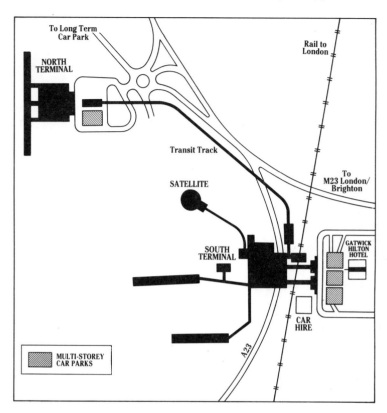

Dia S2.2 London/Gatwick Airport parking.

S3 Manchester

Manchester is a rapidly expanding airport so any list of user airlines may soon become out of date. Listed below are those operators using the airport in 1988 together with their flight prefixes and same day enquiry telephone numbers.

To avoid repeating telephone numbers they are coded as shown below:—

A 061-489 2510
B 061-489 3351
C 061-489 3238/9

For Dan Air   061-489 3321 Arrivals
                061-489 3326 Departures

| Aer Lingus | EI/EIN | Code A |

Aeroflot	SU/AFL	B
Air Canada	AC/ACA	A
Air Ecosse	SM/ECS	C
Air Europa	UX/AEA	A
Air Europe	AE/AEL	A
Air France	AF/AFR	A
Air Furness	GB/AFW	A
Air Malta	KM/AMC	C
Air 2000	AMM	B
American Airlines	AA/AAL	C
Aviaco	AO/AYC	C
Aviogenex	JJ/AGX	C
Balkan-Bulgarian	LZ/LAZ	C
Britannia	BY/BAL	C
British Air Ferries	VF/BAF	C
British Airways	BA/BAW	A
British Island Airways	KD/BIA	C
Cal Air	EN/CAI	A
Caledonian Airways	KT/BKT	A
Connectair	AX/CAX	C
Cyprus Airways	CY/CYP	C
Dan-Air	DA/DAN	
El Al	LY/ELY	C
Guernsey Airlines	GE/GER	C
Hispania	HI/HSL	C
Iberia	IB/IBE	C
Inex Adria	JP/IAA	C
JAT	JU/JAT	C
KAR AIR	KR/KAR	C
KLM	KL/KLM	A
Loganair	LC/LOG	B
LOT Polish Airlines	LO/LOT	A
Manx Airlines	JE/MNX	B
Monarch	OM/MON	B
Qantas	QF/QFA	A
Royal Air Maroc	AT/RAM	C
Ryanair	FR/RYR	C
Sabena	SN/SAB	A
SAS	SK/SAS	A
Singapore Airlines	SQ/SIA	C
Suckling	CB/SAY	A
Swissair	SR/SWR	A
TAP Air Portugal	TP/TAP	C
Tunisair	TU/TAR	C

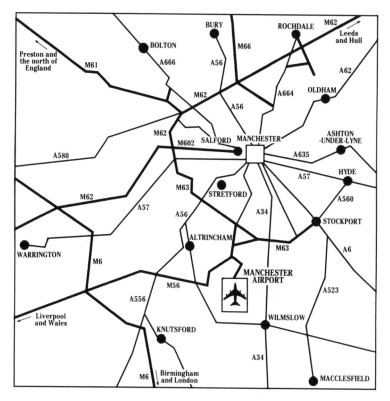

Dia S3.1. Manchester Airport road access.

Wardair	WD/WDA	C
Worldways	WB/WWC	A

Travel to and from the airport by car is not difficult. The M56 motorway goes right up to the entrance and connects within minutes with both the M6 and the M62, Britain's principal north-south and east-west arteries, with links into the national motorway network (Dia S3.1). On the airport follow the signs for car parks or exit or the pick-up or drop-off points (Dia S3.2). Vehicles must not be left unattended and drivers should park in the short stay (multi-storey) car park before meeting or going to see off passengers. A fixed penalty ticket system is in operation for unattended vehicles. Manchester Airport plc advises that for stays of longer than four hours it is cheaper to use the long stay car park.

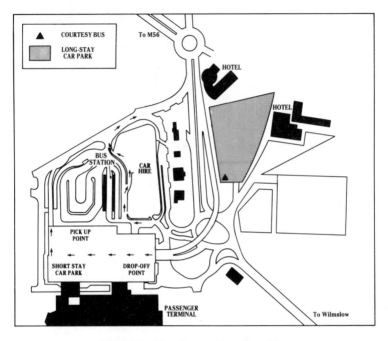

Dia S3.2. Manchester Airport parking.

Public transport consists of local buses between the airport and the bus station, coach station and railway station in Manchester. There are express coach services to towns as far apart as Dundee, Bristol, Taunton and Plymouth and, of course, British Rail services from Manchester can take you all over the country.

Information desks are situated in the main concourse and in the international arrivals hall. They are manned by multi-lingual staff who provide current information on all flight arrivals and departures. They also offer advice on surface transport connections and local hotel accommodation.

A limited area of spectator terracing is open daily during daylight hours; there is no admission charge. There is a souvenir and bookshop and refreshments are available. Tours of the airport are available: telephone 061-499-0303.

S4 Birmingham International

The map in Dia S4.1 says all you need to know about road and rail access for Birmingham International Airport. By road the M6,

M42 and M45 are all within a few miles and, from them, there are direct links to the M1, M5 and M69.

Birmingham International railway station has frequent express train services to Coventry, Wolverhampton, London (Euston)

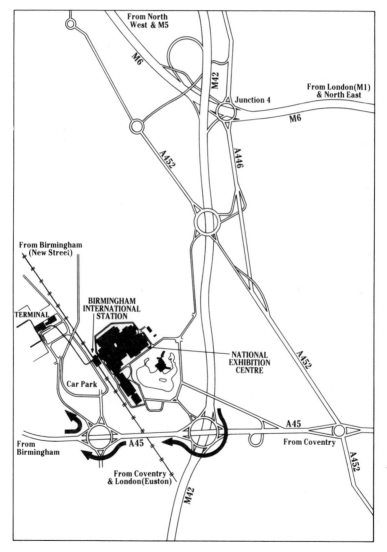

Dia S4.1. Birmingham Airport access and parking.

and Birmingham New Street with its connections to all parts of the country. The fastest journey time to London is 78 minutes and trains run half hourly during the day. Bus services also operate between the terminal and Birmingham city centre. Coventry and Solihull.

There are two handling agencies on the airport so it is convenient to give their flight enquiry telephone numbers and list the airlines for which they are responsible.

BRITISH AIRWAYS   021-767 7503

Adria Airways	JP/ADR
Aer Lingus	EI/EIN
Air France	AF/AFR
Air Atlantis	AIA
British Airways	BA/BAW
Brymon Airways	BC/BRY
Caledonian Airways	KT/BKT
KLM	KL/KLM
Lutfhansa	LH/DLH
Netherlines	WU/NET
NLM	HN/NLM
Swissair	SR/SWR
Tunis Air	TU/TAR
Wardair	WD/WDA
Worldways	WG/WWC

MIDLAND AIRPORT SERVICES   021-767 7704/5

Air Europa	UX/AEA
Air Europe	AE/AEL
Air Malta	KM/AMC
Air Yugoslavia	JR/YRG
Aviogenex	JJ/AGX
Balkan Bulgarian	LZ/LAZ
Birmingham Executive Airways	VB/BEX
Britannia Airways	BY/BAL
British Midland Airways	BD/BMA
Cyprus Airways	CY/CYP
Dan-Air	DA/DAN
Hispania Lineas	HI/HSL
Jersey European Airways	JY/JEA
Jugoslovenski Aerotransport	JU/JAT
Manx Airlines	JE/MNX
Monarch	OM/MON
Paramount	PAT

Ryanair	FR/RYA
Sabena Belgian Airlines	SN/SAB

All you have to do is arrive at the airport, follow signs for car parking and the terminal, or from the train take the MAGLEV link. Inside the terminal follow more signs. It is very straightforward.

Spectators are more than welcome. There is a viewing gallery to which access may be gained by using the lift on the ground floor outside the front of the terminal. A small charge is made and a spotter's shop and buffet are available. There is a very good view of the runways and apron area and many people make use of the facilities for a great family outing. The telephone number is 021-767 7243.

S5 East Midlands International

East Midlands International Airport is only two miles from the M1 Motorway (Junction 24) giving excellent access from areas both to the north and the south. The M42 links the airport to the West Midlands and beyond and there are 'A' class roads to East Anglia and Lincolnshire. It could hardly be easier and you will find that the airport is well signposted. Just follow the signs all the way to the short or long-stay car parks or to the Aeropark, about which more later.

There are direct express coach services to many towns and cities including Ashby, Bedford, Blackpool, Cambridge, Coalville, Derby, Leicester, Loughborough, Manchester, Newmarket, Northampton, Norwich, Nottingham, Preston, Stockport and Stoke-on-Trent. Some of these will have onward connections to other parts of the country. The nearest British Rail stations are at Derby (twelve miles), Loughborough (nine miles), Nottingham (fourteen miles) and Leicester (22 miles).

There are two handling agents on the airport. Their flight enquiry telephone numbers and the airlines they handle are listed below.

SERVISAIR		0332 812278
Air Europa	UX/AEA	
Air Europe	AE/AEL	
Air Yugoslavia	YRG	
Air 2000	AMM	
Aviaco	AO/AYC	
Britannia Airways	BY/BAL	

Caledonian Airways	KT/BKT
Cyprus Airways	CY/CYP
Hispania	HI/HSL
Inex Adria	JP/IAA
Jugoslovenski Aerotransport	JU/JAT
Monarch Airlines	OM/MON
Netherlines	WU/NET
Paramount	PAT
Peregrine	PJ/PSS
Spanair	SPP
TAP Air Portugal	TP/TAP
Tunisair	TU/TAR

BRITISH MIDLAND AIRWAYS   0332 810741

Air Lingus	EI/EIN
Air Malta	KM/AMC
British Midland Airways	BD/BMA
Dan-Air	DA/DAN

A feature of EMA is the Aeropark and Visitor Centre which has become a significant tourist attraction. The Visitor Centre has a number of facilities including displays showing the development of the airport and a history of aviation, as well as a video facility showing how the airport operates. The twelve acre Aeropark site provides tables for family picnics and an excellent view of aircraft using the runway and taxiway. Some refreshments are available.

A range of promotional publications giving details of airport flights and facilities can be obtained by contacting the marketing manager on Derby (0332) 852814.

S6 Leeds/Bradford

Road access to the airport is quite straightforward. The M62 runs east/west a few miles south of the airport and thence from Bradford city centre take the A658, or from Leeds city centre take the A65 to the traffic lights at Rawdon, then the A658. From Skipton take the A65 to the Rawdon traffic lights then left onto the A658; from Harrogate take the A658. Access to the airport and car parks is clearly marked.

When using public transport, hourly bus services operate between Leeds and Bradford and the airport and these are linked by bus and local rail services to other main centres in the region as well as farther afield. There is a continuously occupied taxi rank.

Flight enquiries regarding scheduled services can be made by ringing the numbers listed below:

Aer Lingus	EI/EIN	Leeds 508194
British Midland Airways	BD/BMA	Leeds 508194
Manx	JE/MNX	Leeds 508194
Air UK	UK/UKA	Leeds 503251
Capital	BZ/CPG	Leeds 503251
Wardair	WD/WDA	Leeds 503251
Dan-Air	DA/DAN	Leeds 505650

Holiday and charter flights are usually handled by Servisair, telephone Leeds 503251.

There are two Four Star hotels close by and a 150-bedroom hotel will be built on the airport as part of its future development. Airport spectators are welcome at LBA.

S7 Liverpool

Liverpool airport is easily accessible by road and is well signposted from the nearby M6, M62 and M56 motorways. A bus service links the airport with Garston Station. It operates every fifteen minutes during the day, Monday to Saturday, but half-hourly in the evenings and on Sundays.

From Garston Station trains run frequently to Liverpool City Centre where coaches are available to most major cities in the UK and rail connections may be made for London and the south and Scotland and the north. Runcorn Station, on the main line to Birmingham and the south-west, is a ten-minute taxi journey away.

A considerable number of airlines using Liverpool carry freight or mail and so are not of much interest to the average passenger. The passenger services using the airport are given below. For flight enquiries ring the airport on Liverpool (051) 486 8877.

Aer Lingus	EI/EIN
British Midland Airways	BD/BMA
Jersey European Airways	JY/JEA
Manx Airlines	JE/MNX

Spectators are welcome.

S8 Luton International

There is no need for a map to show how to get to Luton airport by road. Access is via the M1, A1M, M25 or A505; all the routes are well signposted, as are car parks on the airport.

There is plenty of public transport. Luton BR station is served by fast and frequent trains from Kings Cross, St Pancras and Moorgate stations in London (fastest journey time 25 minutes) and Inter-City 125s from Derby, Nottingham, Leicester and Sheffield. There are excellent bus services from the town centre bus station (adjacent to the railway station) as well as coach services to London and many other parts of the country.

The resident airlines at Luton are Britannia and Monarch. It makes sense, then, for those airlines to act as handling agents for other airport users. In the following list of user airlines the flight enquiry telephone numbers are coded as:

| B Britannia Airways | | 0582 424155 |
| M Monarch Airlines | | 0582 424211 |

Air Bridge	AK/ABR	0582 452272
Air Europe	AE/AEL	Code M
Air Malta	KM/AMC	B
Altair	SM	M
Aviaco	AO/AYC	M
Balkan Bulgarian	LZ/LAZ	M
Britannia	BY/BAL	B
British Air Ferries	VF/BAF	B
British Island Airways	KD/BIA	M
British Midland Airways	BD/BMA	B
Dan-Air	DA/DAN	M
Inex Adria	JP/IAA	M
JAT	JU/JAT	M
Monarch	OM/MON	M
TAP Air Portugal	TP/TAP	M
Tunis Air	TU/TAR	M

Spectators are very welcome at Luton airport. They will find a separate, specially designed building with an excellent view of the runway and having a bar and buffet. There is a pay-and-display car park.

S9 Newcastle International

This is another airport which is easy to find. From Newcastle take the city's Central Motorway East and join the A696 at the Cowgate roundabout; from other directions join the A696. The airport is clearly signposted, as are the car parks.

Buses run from the Central railway station at thirty minutes past each hour, calling at Eldon Square before running non-stop to the airport. Express coaches also call at the airport from some fairly far-flung places. Newcastle Central Station provides access to or from all parts of the country.

For flight enquiries just ring the airport and tell the operator which flight you wish to enquire about. Tyneside (091) 286 0966. The user airlines with their prefixes are listed below:

Adria Airways	JP/ADR
Aviaco	AO/AYC
Aviogenex	JJ/AGX
Air Atlantis (TAP)	TP/AIA
Air France	AF/AFR
Air Malta	KM/AMC
Air Europa	UX/AEA
Air UK	UK/UKA
British Airways	BA/BAW
British Island Airways	KD/BIA
Britannia	BY/BAL
Balkan Bulgarian	LZ/LAZ
Caledonian Airways	KT/BKT
Cyprus Airways	CY/CYP
Dan-Air	DA/DAN
Gill Aviation	GIL
Guernsey Airlines	HW/GER
Hispania	HI/HSL
Jugoslovenski Air Transport	JU/JAT
KLM	KL/KLM
Manx	JE/MNX
Oasis	AAN
Paramount	PAT
Spanair	NR/SPP
TAP	TP/TAP
Torosair (Turkish)	TAU
Universair	UN/UNA
Wardair	WD/WDA
Worldways	WG/WWC

The roof terrace is open to spectators throughout the year. A buffet is available during the summer months.

S10 Glasgow

The nearest railway station to Glasgow airport is Paisley Gilmour Street which is two miles from the airport. Main line British Rail connections can be made from here to most parts of the country.

There is a coach service to Glasgow City Centre (Central and Queen Street Stations and Anderston Cross and Buchanan Bus Stations) from the Terminal forecourt every thirty minutes. These coaches also provide an hourly connecting service to Edinburgh City Centre. Buses to Paisley every ten minutes.

By road, access to the airport is via the M8 Motorway (Junction 28) and it will take about twenty minutes from the centre of Glasgow. There is adequate short term and long term car parking. Follow the signs. Car hire desks are in the Domestic Arrivals hall.

For flight enquiries within 24 hours of travel, have the flight number and destination or departure airport ready and telephone (041) 887 1111 Ext 4552.

For further information on airlines listed below you should contact:

British Airways	BA/BAW	(041) 332 9666
Aeroflot	SU/AFL	
LOT	LO/LOT	
Monarch	OM/MON	
British Midland Airways	BD/BMA	(041) 887 1111 Ext 4333
Dan-Air	DA/DAN	(041) 848 4333
Air 2000	AMM	
Loganair	LC/LOG	(041) 887 1111 Ext 4253
Manx Airlines	JE/MNX	
SAS Scandinavian Airlines	SK/SAS	(041) 887 1111 Ext 4239/4330
Serviceair Ltd		(041) 887 1111 Ext 4227
Agent for:		
Adria Airways	JP/ADR	
Aer Lingus	EI/EIN	
Air Bridge	AK/ABR	
Air Ecosse	SM/ECS	

Air Europa	UX/AEA
Air Europe	AE/AEL
Air France	AF/AFR
Air Malta	KM/AMC
Air Portugal	TP/TAP
Air UK	UK/UKA
Aviaco	AO/AYC
Aviogenex	JJ/AGX
Balair	BB/BBB
Balkan Bulgarian	LZ/LAZ
Britannia Airways	BY/BAL
British Air Ferries	VF/BAF
British Island Airways	KD/BIA
Calair	EN/CAI
Canafrica	NCR
Capital Airlines	BZ/CPG
Cyprus Airways	CY/CYP
Guernsey Airlines	GE/GER
Hispania	HI/HSL
Iberia	IB/IBE
Icelandair	FI/ICE
Inex Adria	IAA
JAT	JU/JAT
KLM	KL/KLM
Lufthansa	LH/DLH
Maersk Air	DM/DMA
Martinair	MP/MPH
Oasis	AAN
Paramount	PAT
Ryanair	FR/RYR
Spanair	NR/SPP
Spantax	BX/BXS
Sterling	NB/SAW
Swissair	SR/SWR
Tarom	RO/ROT
Trans Europa	TR/TEU
Transavia	HV/TRN
Tunis Air	TU/TAR
Universair	UN/UNA

There are no spectator facilities at Glasgow airport.

Part 6

We have heard enough about ATC and Part 6 consists of a few comments by the author (every dog has its day) and some appendices. I hope that readers have found the book informative and interesting and that an understanding of the operation has helped to soothe the apprehensions that many have about flying. My own feeling is that this is the quickest and safest way to travel but, oh dear, it can be so boring for the passenger. It is a fascinating job for ATCOs, though.

Author's note

Now I have a problem. The idea of the book was to explain ATC methods and procedures but one can hardly do that without referring to those who practice the art. Since it is an art I hope that in fairness to ATCOs I have not made it appear too much like a routine job that anyone can cope with.

Will grandma now apply to become an ATCO? Does she, or anyone else think that it is just a matter of sitting around saying things like 'Roger, out' or GABCD you are cleared for take-off'? She, or they, would be wrong.

The people selected to look after, and be responsible for, the safety of aircraft both on the ground and in the air, must show before acceptance that they have some experience in aviation which is relevant to the task and/or that they have the educational qualifications which indicate that they could endure the intensive training which they would have to undergo. Interviews are part of the process of sorting out those who have the background and the interest to make them suitable candidates and many fail to impress at this stage. There is not much hope for the candidate who says that he wants to be an ATCO because the pay is good but shows no other interest in the job.

The intensive training is a course, or series of courses, at the College of ATC at Hurn. Students learn such things as navigation, meteorology, air legislation, radio and radar theory and ATC equipment, before going on to aerodrome control, approach control and approach radar control and finally to procedural area control and area radar control. They are also sent to flying schools to learn to fly up to Private Pilot's Licence standard.

The first part of the course is difficult but most get through because, as they have already shown, they have the ability to learn. The problems start with aerodrome control because this is where the practical training starts to come in. Not only practical work, though. There is an awful lot of bookwork in every one of the courses and students have to work very hard from week one because there are progress tests every week in addition to written, oral and practical examinations at the end of each phase. These end of phase examinations must all be passed before going on to the next phase but limited re-sits may be allowed.

Words, regulations and so on can be learned. What cannot be learned is aptitude for the practical work. There seems to be no way of testing this aptitude at the selection stage because there is so much background knowledge to be applied. Sadly, some are now seen not to have the feel for the job. It is no reflection on them when their training is discontinued; after all, we could not all learn to play the piano. It is sadder still if they get to the final course and simply can't come to grips with area radar control. All that application and dedication wasted.

Failure rates are high, usually about thirty per cent. And not all on the practical side, of course. It has been said that the course is too intensive but others think that students who cope with such pressure in training will be less affected by operational pressures later in their careers.

But, as I explained when writing about Gatwick, the training and examinations are not over yet. When students complete the Hurn courses and are presented with their basic licences they are posted to airports or ATCCs and they then have to work for their validations under operational conditions. Although at Hurn students are examined by ATCOs from the CAA Licensing Branch, at the operational units they are trained and examined by people who might have to work with them and validations have to be earned on that basis. Some do not validate.

So it really is not a job for your average grandma. It is not even a job for the average person who is industrious and intelligent because of the aptitude factor.

You may think that this is a task which really should be done by a computer but, strangely, there has not been too much research into this possibility. There was a proposal by the Federal Aviation Authority (FAA) in the USA for an En Route Air Traffic Control Concept using computers but an independent investigation concluded that the concept would require 'virtually perfect software and a complex fail-safe design'. In other words, absolutely no possibility of the sort of error that can cause a computer to churn out a bill for £100,000 when it should be £10.00 plus a total safeguard against any problem with, or failure of, the equipment or the power supplies.

Is there such a computer? Perhaps not and, since we could not contemplate any degree of failure because the human controller would have lost the practice he needs to stay on top of the job and would be unable to retrieve a situation if the computer hiccupped, we would not take chances with the safety of aircraft and lives. So an ATCO monitoring a computer operation is not on.

What might appear some day is a computer that can monitor an ATCO, but my personal view is that even that is unlikely. There are so many variables which cannot be fed into a computer but which the brain can absorb. To the aptitude which is so necessary for ATCOs there is often added a certain instinct and I do not know how you give that to a computer. Obviously, computers must be used for the rapid execution of routine tasks but the greatest resource in the control of aircraft is the Air Traffic Control Officer.

So much for ATCOs. Some laymen will say that the way I have described their job is too bland. What about the emergencies, the flying accidents and so on? The truth is that the job is exciting; controllers work under great pressure because traffic within the system cannot be stopped. Aircraft surging up an airway or taking off and entering the TMA must continue and some have to descend, others to climb, some go here, some go there, all in a controlled and very disciplined environment and the ATCO must accept the responsibilities for his/her part of the operation. They are not allowed to have 'off days' or knock off for a break unless relieved by a fully qualified ATCO. But many can go through their whole careers without experiencing an actual emergency situation.

Even so, it is a lucky controller who does not believe at some time that he does have an emergency on his hands. If a pilot reports a danger indication in the aircraft, that is an emergency situation and it must be handled as such. The aircraft must be given priority and the way cleared for an immediate landing at the nearest available airport. This could well turn out to be an electrical fault in a lighting circuit but no assumptions can be made, the right action must be taken; the adrenalin flows. Again, this does not happen often, but when it does it can affect a whole series of controllers from the en route sectors through to TMA, approach control and aerodrome control, so the grey hairs are spread around a bit.

Because of such possibilities, real or not, the public could not be welcomed into ATC units but it is hoped that this book has helped people to understand what happens when they fly and to give them confidence in the system and those who operate it.

Appendix 1
Aircraft Altitudes

We all know that aircraft carry altimeters which indicate altitude to pilots. For most people, that says it all, but it is an over-simplification and may not even be quite true. For those who have heard such expressions as Flight Level (FL), QNH or QFE and wonder what it is all about, this appendix provides a fuller explanation.

If you have ever seen a weather chart on TV or in a newspaper you will appreciate that atmospheric pressure at mean sea level (msl) varies from place to place (Highs and Lows) and over time (the systems move around). That is the first point to be understood. The second is that an altimeter works on atmospheric pressure and, as an aircraft climbs and the air pressure decreases, the hands of the altimeter rotate like a clock to show the pilot how high he is.

The problem here is that, as we know, the msl pressure is variable so above what datum or starting point will the altimeter indicate? The answer is any datum you like.

Let us relate this to something familiar — the length of a skirt. We can say that a skirt is so many inches above the knee, above the floor or any point or level between the two. All we are doing is relating to a datum. We can do much the same thing with an altimeter. Decide on a level above which we want it to read (the runway =knee, floor =msl), set the atmospheric pressure for that datum and the instrument will indicate altitudes or heights above it. Altimeters have verniers on which any pressure can be set.

There are three levels which interest a pilot. For approach and landing he will want to know his height above the runway, so ATC advises the atmospheric pressure at runway level, the pilot sets it on his altimeter and he can then see how high he is relative to the runway. This pressure is called QFE.

For flights away from airports where the pilot uses a map which shows the elevation of the ground above msl, he will need to set the msl pressure so that his altimeter relates to the map and indicates altitudes amsl which allows him to avoid high ground. This setting is referred to as QNH.

Of course, on a long flight the pressure can vary considerably so the country is divided into Altimeter Setting Regions and the Met Office issues hourly Regional QNHs to be used by all transit aircraft outside controlled airspace. These (forecast) QNHs err on the side of safety and aircraft will invariably be a little higher than is indicated on the altimeter.

So there we have two different altimeter settings, both to do with what is called terrain clearance. The third is different in that it relates aircraft to each other and is concerned only with the separation of aircraft.

If pilots are flying on airways or in holding patterns in TMAs it is vital that their altimeters should all relate to the same datum and, therefore, to each other. (Remember that standard vertical separation is 1000ft; this must not be eroded.) This was achieved by computing an average msl pressure for the whole world (1013.2 mbs 29.92 ins) and using it as a datum for all such aircraft. It is known as the Standard Pressure Setting and the altitudes above which it is to be used are published in aeronautical documents. To avoid confusion, aircraft flying on QNH use altitudes, but aircraft using the Standard Setting refer to their 'vertical displacement' as Flight Levels (FL).

Regardless of the pressure set on the vernier, the altimeter indication will always be in feet. When the pilot is talking Flight Levels on Standard Pressure he will simply take off the last two figures so 8000 is FL80 and 37000ft is FL370. Conversely, a pilot cleared to climb to FL190 will climb to 19,000ft indicated Going back to Chapter 12 where we have drawings of radar screens, you can see that FLs are shown on the secondary radar data blocks.

For those who wish to follow it through, aircraft on airways or in holding stacks use the Standard Setting. When cleared below stack levels they will be given the aerodrome (local) QNH and when aircraft are turned onto final approach the QFE is advised.

Altitudes have been used throughout the book for the same reason that your pilot will refer to an altitude when he welcomes you aboard and tells you the flight plan, namely that most passengers will identify more easily with altitudes.

Just for those who want to know, some countries measure pressures in millibars, some in inches, and their altimeters use the same units. Controllers know who uses which, but either is available on request. Some countries use QNH for landing but, when this is done, runway elevation amsl will be passed at the same time. In the UK (but not in all countries) Standard Pressure is used for flights above 3000ft outside controlled airspace to facilitate a form of separation based on direction of flight. This also means that if an aircraft wishes to cross an airway, the pilot is using the same datum as those on the airway. Pilots and ATCOs need to know a little more than that but you can be sure that they know all they need to know and there are no ambiguities in the system.

Appendix 2

Glossary of Abbreviations

APC	Approach Control
ASMI	Aerodrome Surface Movement Indicator
ATC	Air Traffic Control
ATCC	Air Traffic Control Centre
ATCO	Air Traffic Control Officer
BAA	British Airports Authority
CAA	Civil Aviation Authority
CCTV	Closed Circuit Television
CTA	Control Area
CTR	Control Zone
DFTI	Distance From Touchdown Indicator
DME	Distance Measuring Equipment
EMA	East Midlands Airport
FL	Flight Level
FPS	Flight Progress Strip
GA	General Aviation
GCA	Ground Controlled Approach
GMC	Ground Movement Control
GMP	Ground Movement Planning
ICAO	International Civil Aviation Organization
ILS	Instrument Landing System
LARS	Lower Airspace Radar Service
LATCC	London Air Traffic Control Centre
L/B	Leeds/Bradford Airport
LTMA	London Terminal Control Area
MNR	Minimum Noise Route
msl	mean sea level
MTMA	Manchester Terminal Control Area
NAT	North Atlantic Track
NATS	National Air Traffic Control Services
NDB	Non-Directional Beacon
OACC	Oceanic Area Control Centre
QFE	Barometric pressure at aerodrome level

QNH	Barometric pressure at mean sea level
RASA	Radar Advisory Service Area
RT	Radio Telephone
SBA	Standard Beam Approach
SCATCC	Scottish Air Traffic Control Centre
SFC	Surface
SID	Standard Instrument Departure Route
SRA	Special Rules Area
SRZ	Special Rules Zone
SSR	Secondary Surveillance Radar
STOL	Short Take-Off and Landing
TMA	Terminal Control Area
UK	United Kingdom
VCR	Visual Control Room
VHF	Very High Frequency
VOR	VHF Omni-directional Range (a radio navigation beacon)

Appendix 3

The ICAO phonetic alphabet

A	ALPHA	N	NOVEMBER
B	BRAVO	O	OSCAR
C	CHARLIE	P	PAPA
D	DELTA	Q	QUEBEC
E	ECHO	R	ROMEO
F	FOXTROT	S	SIERRA
G	GOLF	T	TANGO
H	HOTEL	U	UNIFORM
I	INDIA	V	VICTOR
J	JULIETTE	W	WHISKY
K	KILO	X	X-RAY
L	LIMA	Y	YANKEE
M	MIKE	Z	ZULU